Base Jumping

Base Jumping

The Vagabond Life of a Military Brat

BY

WILLIAM WILLIS

Base Jumping: The Vagabond Life of a Military Brat

William Willis Books
11603 Wild Thicket
San Antonio, Texas 78254
210-218-6505
http://www.williamwillisbooks.com
info@williamwillisbooks.com

ISBN 978-0-9894052-0-1

Cover Design: Aundrea Hernandez
Author Photo: Lee Byrd
Editors: Lillie Ammann, Jan McClintock

Dedication

In loving memory of my parents,
Sidney and Doris Willis
and…
for Jan

Acknowledgements

I would like to express my gratitude to those who encouraged me in this new endeavor and read my first rough draft. Foremost my wife, Carrie, took the time to offer valuable advice and point out numerous errors. My longtime friend, Aurora Freeman, shared her great proofreading skills and suggestions. I especially want to thank my friend and fellow writer, David Bowles (the Westward Sagas), who wasn't afraid to tell me what I needed to hear instead of what I wanted to hear.

Producing a quality book would be impossible without the assistance of a great editor. I was fortunate in that regard to have Lillie Ammann and her assistant, Jan McClintock, in my corner. I would like to thank them for their technical expertise and sage advice.

Since my parents are gone, I relied heavily on Uncle William and Aunt Ruby Frier and Aunt Helen Compton to provide dates and details on important events. To them I express my heartfelt love and appreciation.

Introduction

This book is about my childhood and what it was like growing up in a military household. It wasn't until I was in my teens that I realized that our family life was quite different than that of civilian families. As a kid, I accepted my father's abrupt disappearances for months at a time as just a normal part of life. I later found out that while we were safe at home in our beds, Dad was risking his life spying on our biggest Cold War enemy along communist Russia's border.

Mom was given the standard explanation all intelligence officers gave their wives: "Don't worry, it's just temporary duty. I'll be home soon." We hated to see him leave, but he always remembered to bring us wonderful presents from the strange, faraway places he visited.

When Dad was home, one of our cherished family rituals was "story time" at the dinner table. This ritual usually took place after our Sunday meal. While Mom prepared dessert, Dad sat back and launched into another story of the "good old days." Mom would occasionally toss in a few nuggets, but Dad brought the past to life. Oh boy, could he tell a great story! He would get that gleam in his eyes and, within minutes, we would be transported back in time to Prentiss Avenue in Portsmouth, Virginia, during the Great

Depression or the dark days of World War II and the post-war years. Sometimes, Dad and Mom included interesting stories about their parents and brothers and sisters.

At the beginning of each chapter, I'll relate one of these amazing and wonderful tales under the heading A Dinner Tale. I asked Dad many times to write these stories down for future generations. He never did. I've come to the realization that since both my parents, as well as my older sister Jan are gone, it's up to me to keep these memories alive.

Prologue

The pilot edged the great lumbering C-130 Hercules closer to Russian air space, mindful of the fact that accidentally straying over the border could mean instant death. Russian MiG fighter planes patrolled constantly under orders from Moscow to shoot down any foreign aircraft suspected of conducting espionage missions against their country, precisely what the C-130 and its intelligence-gathering crew known as "back-enders" was doing.

On board was an air crew consisting of six flight crew members (the "front-enders") and eleven reconnaissance specialists (the "back-enders") who monitored Soviet bloc communications. The two halves of the crew were kept separate by a locked door and reported to different headquarters. Though the flight crew possessed secret and top secret clearances, due to the sensitive nature of the back-enders' activities, the flight crew was kept in the dark as to the true nature of the mission. Their job was to fly the plane anywhere they were instructed, without question. The flight crew may have guessed what the back-enders were up to but did not officially know who they were or why the pilot was ordered to fly a specific route.

One of the back-enders was a young Air Force officer whose training as a cryptologist made him keenly aware of the importance of this mission. A World War II veteran with thirty-two missions as a B-17 top turret gunner over Nazi Germany, Captain Sidney Augustine Willis was no stranger to the fear and perils of combat.

He grew up a scrappy kid in depression-era Portsmouth, Virginia. He had never backed down from a fight and wasn't about to now. That boldness, however, didn't stop his hands from shaking as he lit another Camel cigarette. What would happen to his wife and kids should something go wrong today? Trying to banish those negative thoughts from his mind, he turned his attention to the task at hand—intercepting and recording Russian radio transmissions.

The Russians and the Americans had been spying on each other since World War II ended and the Cold War started, and Captain Willis was in the thick of it.

"Captain, it looks like we've got a visitor," the pilot nervously announced over the intercom.

The young intelligence officer snubbed out his cigarette and peered out the starboard window. A Russian MiG was no more than fifty feet away, its pilot glaring back at him with a menacing look on his face. Seconds later, in a radio transmission, the Russian threatened to shoot down the C-130 if it came any closer to Russian air space.

After making eye contact with the Russian pilot, the young officer gave his nemesis that special Sid Willis grin accompanied by a patriotic one-finger salute. "Let's wrap it up and go home," he replied to the pilot. "We've done enough damage for one day."

With trembling fingers, he lit another cigarette and tried to relax. *Just another day at the office,* he thought to himself.

One

A Dinner Tale

As in many small towns across Depression-era America, money for entertainment was scarce. For that reason, many people gravitated to the public places where they found acceptance and friendship. Dad's father owned a small barber shop that was one of those places, and it didn't take long for it to become a hub of social activity.

Granddad was a popular figure in the neighborhood. Some visitors came for haircuts, but most dropped by for camaraderie with their neighbors. Though not well-educated, Granddad was intelligent and well-read. He dispensed wisdom and advice (as well as free haircuts to the Depression-era unemployed who were unable to pay) as readily as he did the hair tonics gracing his countertops. For this reason, friends and neighbors respectfully referred to him as Cap'n instead of his given name, Jewell.

One day, the local beat cop dropped in and insisted on showing Granddad the latest unbreakable hold he had just learned. "Hey, Cap'n, I gotta show you this new hold they taught us. It's impossible for anyone to escape from it."

Granddad was busy cutting someone's hair and had a few more customers lined up, so he said, "Come back later, will you? Can't you see I'm busy?"

"Come on, Cap'n. It'll just take a minute," the cop insisted. "I really want you to see it. No one's ever been able to break it."

"Not now. Show me later."

The cop pleaded, but to no avail. Finally, he said, "Okay, Cap'n, I'll come back later."

Instead of leaving, however, he snuck up behind Granddad and quickly grabbed his arm and twisted it behind his back while putting him in a chokehold.

Granddad yelled, "Let me go, goddammit!"

"You can't get loose, can you?" the cop asked triumphantly.

"I'm only going to tell you one more time. Let… me…go!" Granddad warned.

The cop just laughed as did everyone else in the shop. It ended a minute later when Granddad spun around, escaping the "unbreakable hold," and hauled off and punched the cop square in the face, knocking him flat on his back.

When the cop finally staggered to his feet, rubbing his jaw, he meekly said, "Well, gotta get going, Cap'n. I'll see you around."

As the embarrassed cop walked out the door amid the nervous laughter of the other patrons, Granddad called out, "If you come up with any more of those unbreakable holds, you be sure and let me know, okay?"

The cop was a beefy, young member of Portsmouth's finest. Granddad was around five-foot-six and couldn't *have weighed more than one hundred and thirty pounds soaking wet. I understand why everyone called him Cap'n.*

❧

I stood off to the side of the Kelly Air Force Base runway with my fingers entwined in the chain link fence, watching in awe as the F-100 fighter jet came in for a smooth three-point landing. I had spent the better part of the morning watching the succession of sleek F-100 and F-102 jets and the big-bellied C-130 Hercules cargo planes practice their takeoffs and landings. I was captivated by this aeronautical playground and fantasized that I was at the controls of those beautiful machines.

I burst through the kitchen screen door, nearly knocking it off its hinges. "I know what I want to be someday." I had to stop and catch my breath after sprinting through the weed-filled vacant lot separating our house from the runway, barely a stone's throw away.

"Don't tell me. A trumpet player?" Mom asked, with an affectionate smile.

"Nah, that's for sissies," I answered.

She was alluding to my interest in learning to play the trumpet that Dad had recently bought for me on one of his many trips abroad.

"I'm going to be a jet pilot," I added.

Her face fell, and I knew I had struck a nerve. Dad wanted me to join the Air Force, but Mom was dead set on discouraging me from joining the military. She had tried her best to make me realize how tough that sort of life could be on a family: the constant moving and countless separations.

"We've talked about this before, Bill," she said, caressing my face with her hand. "I want you to go to college and get a regular job and raise a family in one place."

"I'm just kidding, Mom," I lied.

I didn't want to hurt her, but I wanted to be inside one of those cockpits so bad I could almost taste it.

"When is Dad coming home?" I asked, trying to change the subject.

"I don't know."

"Where is he?" I persisted.

"I don't know that either. Don't you have some homework to do?" She turned away but not before I saw tears forming in her eyes.

I went to my room and picked up the B-17 model airplane Dad had helped me put together before he left.

He had pointed out the top turret canopy with its twin 50-caliber machine guns. "That's where I sat while flying thirty-two combat missions over Nazi Germany during World War II," he said, with immense pride. "My job was to protect our plane from the German Luftwaffe fighter aircraft during our bombing runs. It was thirteen years ago, but I still have nightmares of seeing some of the other B-17s in our formation being shot down. The worst part was seeing other crewmembers bailing out with their parachutes on fire, knowing they were falling to their deaths."

Dad was not only my hero, he was also my buddy and we were extremely close. I held the model airplane aloft as I ran around my room imagining I was with Dad helping him blast away at the German fighters. I tripped and the B-17 went cartwheeling through the air, landing with a crash and splintering into a hundred pieces. Instead of picking up the mess, I crawled into bed and cried myself to sleep, wondering where Dad was and when he was coming home. I was eight years old.

Two

A Dinner Tale

Granddad decided to teach Dad and his older brother, Ben, the joys and importance of hard work. For each of them, he made a shoeshine kit equipped with shoe polish, polishing rags, brushes, and a wooden box that doubled as a storage case and a footrest for their customers. After getting them spruced up, with their hair combed, he stationed them at the end of a long bench in the waiting area of the barber shop. Here they patiently waited for prospective customers.

When the first man walked in and took a seat on the bench, Granddad glanced over at Uncle Ben and gave him an imperceptible nod. Ben jumped into action and, with kit in hand and a big smile on his face, walked over to the man and asked, "Would you like a shoeshine, sir?"

Unable to resist this eager, industrious young boy, he replied, "Sure, kid."

Granddad then smiled his approval at Uncle Ben.

After a while, another man entered the shop and took a seat. Again, Granddad glanced over and gave another imperceptible nod, this time to Dad. Instead of jumping up as Grandpa expected, Dad scowled and gave a slight shake of his head.

Exasperated, Granddad fixed his steely eyes on Dad and rolled his eyes in the direction of the man, followed by another shake of the head. This odd exchange went on several more times, until Dad finally dragged himself off the bench, and, frowning, slowly approached the man, who seemed to be amused by the whole affair.

With all the enthusiasm of a prisoner facing the gallows, he asked, "You don't want a shoeshine, do you, sir?"

Not surprisingly, the man replied, "No, thanks, kid."

Acting as if he had just received a full pardon, Dad then bounded back to the end of the bench and sat down with a triumphant grin. Granddad, in frustration, walked over, took the shoeshine kit from his indolent son and told him to go on home. Dad's shoeshine career started and ended the same day.

In 1945, shortly after World War II ended, Dad left the Army Air Corps and returned to Portsmouth, Virginia, where he found work as an apprentice mechanic at the Naval Shipyard in Norfolk. Mom was a high school dropout working as a soda jerk at the local drug store soda counter. He was twenty-two and she was seventeen. After dating for a few months, they married on December 8, 1945. They didn't make much money and lived from paycheck to paycheck in a small apartment. My parents couldn't afford a car, so Dad hitchhiked to and from work each day, which wasn't easy considering he was usually covered in oil and grease. Luckily for him, hitchhiking was a common mode of transportation in those trying times.

My sister, Janice, and I were both born in Portsmouth. She made her debut on September 27, 1946, and I made my entrance on December 6, 1949. Dad had re-enlisted in 1946 in the Army Air Corps (now known as the Air Force) a year after his discharge because of the poor job market. He lost a stripe and a pay grade, but at least it was a steady job with a future.

When I was six months old, we transferred to San Antonio, Texas. We lived in an apartment over a garage on the south side while Dad was stationed at Kelly Air Force Base. After considerable thought, he decided that the only way he would stay in the Air Force was if he could become an officer. Supporting a growing family on an enlisted man's pay was difficult. I mentioned earlier that he had taken a pay cut when he re-enlisted—such a nice way to reward one of our returning war heroes. He applied and was accepted to the Reserve Officers Candidate School. He breezed through that and became a brand new second lieutenant. With those gold bars, a pay raise, and his self-confidence, he stood ready to take on the world, committed to making the Air Force his career.

Soon after his promotion, we transferred to Chanute Air Force Base in Rantoul, Illinois. That's where my earliest memories were formed. Since it took about a year to get on-base housing, my parents rented a small farmhouse fifteen miles outside of town.

I vaguely remember our place being surrounded by miles of flat farmland.

My first memory was of being awakened in the morning in my crib by a loud mooing coming from the living room. One of our neighbor's cows had decided to pay us a visit by sticking her head in one of our open windows.

After six months of living in the country, we moved into a small house a little closer to town. I knew we were still somewhat out in the countryside, because we were still surrounded by farmland. A crop field behind our house was bordered on the far side by a train track. I spent hours sitting on the back porch watching trains pass by or wandering between the rows of crops, watching the farmers drive big green tractors. I was fascinated with the way the front wheels angled inward in the shape of a V and with the odd-looking plows they dragged behind them. These early memories are why I have such a sentimental reaction to the sight of trains and green tractors.

Mom took me on a shopping trip to the department store in town. Dad had our only car, so Mom said we would take the bus. I had no memory of ever riding on a bus, so it was a new experience for me. I remember a huge vehicle pulling up to the curb, and, as the driver opened the door, I glanced back and saw a gigantic dog painted on its side.

This was the first time I had ever seen a Greyhound bus. Because I thought the dog was real, I started screaming in terror. Mom picked me up and practically threw me on the bus; however, I didn't get on without a fight. Mom had a tough time trying to pry my fingers and feet off the door frame. I was convinced we were going to be eaten alive.

Judging by the irritated look on the driver's face, I think he was considering taking off without us. Eventually I calmed down, when Mom convinced me it was just a picture of a dog.

Later, while walking through the store, I spotted the candy counter and asked Mom for some candy. "Hand me my purse," she said. Unfortunately, in her infinite wisdom, she had entrusted her four-year-old son with holding her purse while she was trying on shoes.

"I don't have it," I replied, innocently, realizing I'd probably laid it down while looking at toys.

"What do you mean, you don't have it?" she yelled. From the furious and panicked look on her face, I thought she was going to smack me clear across the lingerie department.

After retracing our steps, we never did find her purse, and now, thanks to me, there was no money, no driver's license, no military ID, and none of whatever other stuff she kept in that purse. Did I mention no candy, either? That was the worst part, as far as I was concerned.

Several months later, we were approved for on-base housing. On-base housing was great, because we were closer to everything: the PX (post exchange), commissary, hospital, pool, playgrounds, movie theater—all the typical amenities that make an Air Force Base a self-contained community. I remember moving into a beautiful red-brick, two-story house with a big yard.

My memories of living here are vague. One incident that stands out involved my deciding for some reason to run full-speed, headfirst through the living room plate glass window. Miraculously, I didn't suffer a single scratch.

I sat on the floor and watched the repairman install the new pane of glass. He looked at me and said, "Your mother told me you broke this window. How did you do it?"

"With my head," I replied, as if he couldn't have asked a dumber question.

He mumbled something to himself and turned back to the job at hand. I guess he didn't have kids.

Even though I escaped injury this time, it didn't take long for me to become intimately acquainted with the base hospital and its depressingly crowded waiting room. I was a reckless, accident-prone kid and spent a lot of time there getting my head stitched up from my various misadventures.

Dad decided to take me along on one of his hunting trips with his buddy. I nearly froze to death—the temperature sometimes got as low as minus sixty degrees on those flat plains, due to the frigid air blasting across Lake Michigan from Canada. He brought along a 12-gauge shotgun for himself and a smaller .410 shotgun for his friend to use.

He decided that day would be a good day for his five-year-old son to learn to handle a shotgun. He cocked the .410, handed it to me, and told me to aim at a tree. The gun was longer than I was, but I managed to hoist it up to my shoulder. I pulled the trigger and the blast sent me flying backwards, dropping the gun on the way.

When I got up, I noticed my nose was bleeding. I had held the shotgun too close and the recoil sent it backwards into my face. I cried a little, but I think Dad was more proud than worried.

I refused to touch the shotgun after that, but I still enjoyed walking through the fields doing my best to help spot the elusive pheasant we were searching for. I had never heard of a pheasant, but Dad said to look for a large bird about the size of a turkey. He said it was very good eating. He finally bagged one, and we brought this strange-looking bird with long beautiful, colorful feathers home with us.

I watched Dad pluck and dress it. Mom cooked it for dinner that night (after chewing Dad out for letting me shoot his gun), while I played with its tail feathers. The cooked pheasant tasted pretty good.

In 1955, we returned to San Antonio. We moved into an apartment in a military housing complex called Billy Mitchell Village, adjacent to Kelly Air Force Base. We only lived there about a year, but I recall wandering the neighborhood a lot without much supervision. Dad usually either worked or golfed, and Mom spent most of her time taking care of my new baby brother, Buddy. Jan had her own friends and didn't want her little brother tagging along.

A big pasture adjoined our neighborhood (the site where John F. Kennedy High School now stands). A huge bull was fenced there, and my friend and I liked to cross the field and sneak up on it to see who could get the closest without it noticing us. It was a dumb thing to do, considering it could have turned on us in a second and made mincemeat out of us. Luckily, the bull was more interested in munching grass than chasing down a couple of crazy kids.

One of the highlights of living in San Antonio in 1955 was attending my first rodeo, the *6th Annual San Antonio Stock Show and Rodeo*. This rodeo was fairly new but would become a big part of the entertainment scene in San Antonio. It still brings in huge crowds every February, and, for sentimental reasons, I take my family to it and the accompanying carnival every year. The featured performers that year were Western movie stars Roy Rogers, my boyhood idol, and his wife, Dale Evans. Forever burned in my memory are the two of them galloping towards me during the opening ceremony and, later, singing "Happy Trails."

In 1956, we embarked on another of our many cross-country trips. We were returning to my birthplace: Portsmouth, Virginia. The Air Force was sending Dad to South Korea for a one-year assignment as a squadron commander. He felt it would be better if we moved next door to our grandparents so they could watch over us. Dad knew that raising three youngsters by herself would be difficult for Mom and by being next to his parents, she would be able to count on them for help.

I remember watching Mom cry as my parents said good-bye to each other in front of our new home, the left half of my grandparents' duplex. This memory stands out because I had rarely seen Mom cry like that. Dad was thirty-two and Mom was twenty-seven. It was the first, but definitely not the last, time in their marriage they would be separated by his job.

He was an intelligence officer now and spent a lot more time overseas during the Cold War helping to fight the communism that was spreading throughout the world like a cancer. His training as a cryptologist was demanding an ever-increasing presence in a number of hotspots around the world. His family had no idea what he was doing or where he was at any given time. The work of a cryptologist was classified, and he was forbidden to discuss his job with his family.

A neighbor once asked me if my father was a missionary. I had never heard the term, so I naively responded, "Yeah, I guess so." I received a lot of strange looks (and blessings) from the neighbors after that.

The duplex was a magnificent, two-story structure with a wide front porch. Thick hedges separated the front yard from the sidewalk, and I often sat on the porch steps and watched Granddad trim the hedges as meticulously as he cut his customer's hair. Next door, on the corner, was a one-story building that housed his barber shop and a dry cleaning business operated by my grandmother, whom everyone called Mammy.

A railroad track ran down the middle of the street in front of the barber shop. My cousin Conley and I loved to run alongside the slow-moving trains and wave at the engineers, who tossed us large pieces of chalk they used to mark boxcars. Free chalk was a real treat back then. When we pumped our fists, they rewarded us with a blast of their horn. I mentioned earlier my love affair with trains. I was always the first out the door when I heard that welcome blast of the horn from an approaching train.

As with the previous shop Granddad owned when Dad was a kid, this one also had two swivel chairs and served as a popular meeting place for the locals. I remember playing and spinning around in the chairs and trying out all the exotic-smelling hair tonics while Granddad took care of customers.

With Dad overseas and Mom busy taking care of Buddy, I had free rein to roam the neighborhood without supervision. I engaged in all sorts of mischievous behavior, from pulling the neighbor's laundry off their clothesline to playing with matches. If Dad had been there, there's no way I would have been able to get away with the things I did.

It wasn't long before I had a run-in with the police. Walking home from school one day, I spied some unusual-looking black containers that resembled little cannon balls.

I learned they were smudge pots that road crews would light (they were probably filled with kerosene or some other flammable substance); they were used to keep traffic away from construction projects. I assume they were the precursors of today's road flares.

I refer to them as smudge pots because they looked almost identical to the smudge pots I encountered years later in Florida citrus groves. There, the growers would place them next to the trunks of citrus trees in cold weather and light the wicks to ward off frost damage to their crops.

I thought that, since the smudge pots looked like little cannonballs, it would be fun to bombard the neighbors' porches. I must have "bombed" at least three homes before I heard a police siren behind me. A policeman jumped out of his squad car, chewed me out, then tossed me into the back seat. He drove me home and read Mom the riot act for not being a responsible parent. Even though I got a good whipping, I secretly thought I was hot stuff—how many kids get a police escort home from school?

Grandpa and Grandma Frier often came over and picked Jan and me up to spend weekends with them. They lived in a small house in Cradock, several miles away. Since Grandpa was retired from his railroad job, he and Grandma had unlimited time to spend with their grandkids. These visits gave Mom a much-needed break. We were lucky—many military families didn't have that support system.

Those were tough days for Mom. It was the longest time my parents had been separated from each other. There were occasions, years later, when Dad had to leave on temporary duty for several months at a time, but since we kids were older, and Mom had more experience raising kids, we were easier to handle.

Three

A Dinner Tale

Dad was ordered to fly to post-World War II Germany for several months of temporary duty. No matter where he went, if there was a wild party within a hundred miles he would find it. Foreign countries were no exception.

One night he and his buddies heard about a masquerade party being thrown by the local Germans. Tensions were still a little high among the populace, since the Americans had just bombed the hell out of their country a few years before.

Dad and his friends showed up uninvited and started drinking pretty heavily. They were standing off to the side watching a group of costumed revelers dancing around in a large circle, similar to a conga line. Each participant had his or her hands on the dancer in front, all except for one costumed pair. They were dressed in a horse costume, one person wearing the front half and the other person wearing the back half.

I don't know if it was because Dad was American (most of the spectators were German), but every time the horse would dance by him the person in front would kick him. After a while, he got fed up and decided to *do something about it. The next time around, Dad was waiting for him. Once again, the horse kicked him. This time Dad jumped in front of the horse and hauled off and punched him in the muzzle as hard as he could. He hit him so hard that the horse's head went flying across the room. The horse buckled to the ground, minus its head. The music died, and everyone in the room looked on in shock at the sight before them. Lying there with a dazed look and a sore jaw was a beautiful young German woman.*

Suddenly, a group of German men started yelling and lunged at Dad. Though small, he was fast, and he realized he might have just re-ignited World War II. He disappeared through the nearest exit and hurtled down a long flight of steps with those angry Huns on his tail looking for vengeance.

When Dad burst through the front door of the building, he spied a taxicab at the curb with a young couple about to enter. He jerked them aside and dove into the cab, yelling, "They've got guns, and they're trying to kill me. Go! Go!" After Dad got back, I'm sure he didn't set foot off that base until it was time to return to the States.

After Dad returned from a year-long assignment in Korea in the summer of 1957, our family packed up and headed west. Like some giant magnet, San Antonio was once again pulling us home. Relatives in Virginia thought we were returning to the wild west: a land of cowboys strolling the dusty streets, horses and cows vying for space instead of buses and cars. My friends asked me if we rode horses everywhere. I would have been in heaven had that been the case. Instead, we ended up back in Billy Mitchell Village, just a few buildings away from our previous residence.

Mom enrolled me in Winston Elementary School, located just outside Kelly Air Force Base's north gate. I drove through Billy Mitchell Village recently and was surprised to find that my old neighborhood is now low-income civilian housing instead of quarters for military families.

Jan was eleven years old and in the sixth grade, and Buddy was one year old and just learning to walk. Dad's preoccupation with golf was in full swing, and he spent weekends golfing with his buddies at the old Kelly Golf Course, a small course that was later torn down and replaced by a new course of the same name on the other side of the base. Mom had no hobbies. She spent her time taking care of kids.

While living there, I found out just how dangerous girls could be. There was a playground in our neighborhood with a big swing set. One day, I decided to steal a kiss from a cute girl I liked, so I snuck up behind her, leaned over, and surprised her with a peck on the cheek. She immediately hauled off to smack me, but I jumped back and laughed. She lunged at me for another shot, and, still laughing, I turned and ran directly into the path of a moving swing. The kid in the swing had his back to me and never saw me. The metal seat caught me just outside my right eye and knocked me at least ten feet into a chain link fence.

By now I was the only one not laughing. When the other kids saw the blood dripping from my face, they gathered around and stared in fascination. They must have thought the girl clobbered me. As I ran home crying, I could hear a couple of boys following my bloody trail, pointing at the sidewalk and yelling, "Look… there's a drop of blood." "Oh, look… there's another one."

One doctor's visit and three stitches later, I was home. It took eight years for me to summon up the courage to steal another kiss from a girl, and I made damn sure there weren't any swing sets nearby.

I saw a sign: "$25 Reward for Reporting Vandalism." That was a lot of money, so I devised a plan to get that reward. A friend and I started throwing rocks, and I dared him to break a window in one of the apartments. The moron broke it on the next throw. Like a loyal buddy, I ran into the manager's office to snitch on my friend, giving the manager my friend's name and address and then politely asking for the reward. She didn't believe me and told me to get lost. Not only was there no reward, but also my friend threatened to beat me up for turning him in. I tried to persuade him it wasn't personal and that I was going to split the money with him. He wasn't convinced. We weren't friends after that.

Since Mom didn't have a job, she decided to save money by cutting my hair herself. It sounds ridiculous, but she used a bowl as a guide. I remember sitting outside with a silver-colored metal bowl planted on my head while she started clipping away with her scissors. I'm sure Granddad would have been appalled had he witnessed this travesty.

The lady next door came over, pulled up a chair and, with a suppressed smile, watched the action. A few minutes later, another lady dropped by to join the fun. They gave Mom advice on the proper way to cut hair. After a while, the smiles of the women gave way to snickering.

What the heck's so funny? I wondered. When Mom finally removed the bowl, everyone started laughing, except me. I ran into the house and looked in a mirror. Staring back at me was a seven-year-old Prince Valiant. When Dad got home from work, he took me to the barber shop to repair the damage (after he quit laughing). I refused to let Mom touch my hair after that. So much for trying to save money.

Occasionally, Mom and Dad took us to one of the many city parks that dotted San Antonio. One of our favorites was a small park, Pablo's Grove, just off Old Highway 90 between Kelly and Lackland Air Force Bases. It's still there, but since the new Interstate Highway 90 relegated the Old Highway 90 to a seldom-used back road, the park is hard to find. It's a little run down and goes by a different name now: Mateo Camargo Park. I've driven over there a few times just to walk around and reminisce about the great times Jan, Buddy, and I shared there so many years ago.

My first brush with show business occurred about this time. Every spring, San Antonio celebrates Fiesta. The event was created in 1891 to honor the heroes of the Alamo and San Jacinto, and, for ten days, San

Antonio celebrates this event with a parade down Broadway, a night river parade, and an enormous carnival downtown.

During that time, there were numerous smaller carnivals scattered around town, mostly in shopping center parking lots. At the one that was set up in our neighborhood grocery store parking lot, I was bitten by the carnival bug. It was also there I was nearly trampled by a horse.

Early Saturday afternoon, I elbowed my way to the front of a large crowd to see what all the commotion was. Usually these smaller carnivals had a midway, concession stands, sideshows, and a few rides, but this was different. I saw a ring enclosing a man with a small whip, who I assumed was some sort of ringmaster. He expertly guided two galloping white horses in a counter-clockwise circle around the perimeter of the ring.

I had never seen anything like that before, but what really captured my attention was a beautiful, scantily-dressed girl standing on the back of one the horses. I watched her expertly leap off one horse, do a cartwheel, leap up onto the other horse's back, and execute a few more acrobatic moves. I was mesmerized.

After a few minutes, an announcer asked for two volunteers from the audience. I didn't know what he wanted volunteers for, but if it involved getting next to that half-naked girl, I was in. I shot my hand out and was picked right away along with a girl I recognized from school. He asked if we wanted to ride the horses and, of course, we said yes. I had never been on a horse but had dreamed of riding one ever since I saw Roy Rogers riding Trigger two years previously at the rodeo.

Back then, parental consent forms didn't exist, so workers immediately hooked us up to body harnesses. They were attached to ropes suspended from some sort of crane-like rig in the middle of the ring. I looked up at the top of this rickety-looking contraption about twenty feet in the air and asked, "Uh… what's that stuff for? I thought you said we were just going to ride the horses around in a circle."

"Yeah, you're gonna ride 'em alright," the ringmaster replied with a sly grin. "The harness is so you don't break your fool neck."

"What do you… Whooooa!" I yelled as I felt my body being hoisted up in the air. I looked across the ring and saw my classmate dangling from another rope. I was a little scared but wasn't about to let her know it, so I started waving at the people in the audience. *This ain't so bad*, I thought, after a smattering of applause.

The horses were positioned below us, and we were gently lowered onto their bare backs. The ringmaster prodded the horses into a slow walk. So far so good. Then he used the whip to bring them to a gallop. This was a little harder, but with the harness, I felt reasonably safe. After a few minutes of smiling and waving at the crowd, I heard the announcer say something about doing some trick riding. My ears perked up. *What's that supposed to mean?* I thought. Before I figured it out, I noticed that my horse was sinking. Or to be more exact, I was rising. *What the hell?*

"Keep a hold of the mane and stand on his back," the ringmaster yelled. I looked across the ring and saw my classmate standing perfectly on her horse's back and smiling to thunderous applause.

Not to be outdone, I tried to stand gracefully on this bouncing pile of horseflesh while hanging onto its mane. *Gracefully* and Bill Willis are words rarely used in the same sentence. My arms and legs never did get synchronized. While the girl performed like a pro to cheers and applause, I got hoots and hollers and unbridled (pun intended) laughter. I might have made a lousy Roy Rogers, but I would have made a great rodeo clown.

When it seemed things couldn't get any worse, they did. Whether it was the crane operator speeding up or the horse slowing down, I found myself dangling in front of my horse looking him square in the eye.

Oh great. Being humiliated isn't enough… I'm going to be trampled. I felt like a giant carrot on a stick.

As our faces drew closer and closer together, I felt myself being jerked up even higher. As I hovered five feet above the horse, the announcer yelled, "Stand on his back!" The crane operator was apparently giving me another chance to kill myself.

Since I kind of enjoyed the attention, I decided to do my best to comply. As they lowered me, my feet finally made contact with the horses back, but with a twist. I was now facing backwards. Not to blow my short brush with fame (I was really liking the atten-tion now), I pretended I did it on purpose and waved and smiled at the crowd.

Fate wasn't quite finished with me just yet. Before I had a chance to revel in my new-found glory, I felt myself, once again, being jerked up into the air. Either the crane was malfunctioning, or the operator had a wicked sense of humor. When I looked down for my horse, it wasn't there. I was dangling midway between the two horses, spinning out of control, arms flailing like the blades on a busted windmill.

I guess the announcer must have thought we'd had enough fun and brought the horses to a halt and lowered us to the ground. I felt a combination of embarrassment and euphoria. I finally got to ride a horse… well, sort of, if the definition of the word *ride* was broad enough. I also figured I'd never see any of those people again. The girl was a different story. I threatened her with torture if she ever uttered a word of this to our classmates.

Dad, a fairly new officer, was still gung-ho on the rigorous spit-and-polish training he had received in Officer Candidate School and insisted Jan and I call him "sir." As he aged, Dad mellowed, but in those days he was a strict disciplinarian. Janice, being a girl, didn't fit the military mold, and Buddy was still a baby, so I received the benefit of Dad's unorthodox training. We were a squadron of two: Dad, the squad leader, and I, the lowly recruit. I sometimes felt like I was nothing more than Dad's obedient little soldier.

Dad assigned me tasks that, at the time, I thought were normal for boys my age. I received a salary of $1.25 per month. Dad taught me responsibility by deducting five cents from this amount every time I left a light on, and he taught me the importance of physical conditioning by making me exercise every night before bedtime.

Sometimes, I tried to sneak off to bed when he wasn't looking, but he would always come in later, flick on the light and ask, "Did you do your exercises tonight?"

"No, sir," I would answer meekly. He would then make me get out of bed and do my exercises.

I had to do one hundred push-ups in groups of thirty, thirty, and forty. Then Dad made me lie flat on my back, motionless, while I rested up for the one hundred sit-ups that were to follow. He convinced me that, during the Civil War, General Thomas "Stonewall" Jackson made his men lie down between battles to conserve their energy and I believed him. Later, I realized Dad was full of baloney, but to a seven-year-old boy it sounded plausible. I already mentioned his penchant for tall tales.

This training also extended to our meal-time activities. Dad made Jan and me search the newspaper for current events which we had to read aloud and discuss during dinner. That wasn't too bad, but the spelling and math quizzes that he made us take during the meal caused problems. Mom thought Dad was being unreasonable, but his rules were law in our house.

Even though Jan was three years older, I was better at math and spelling. Consistently out-performed, she sometimes got upset and cried at the table. It wasn't until we were adults that Jan told me of the humiliation she felt and the resentment she harbored toward Dad and me for putting her through that. It wasn't my fault, but she partially blamed me for making her look bad.

As a cadet at the Coast Guard Academy twelve years later enduring the cruel hazing by the officers and upperclassmen, I realized where Dad got this nonsense. It wasn't his fault—he was a young father and junior officer who was so wrapped up in his own world that he thought what worked in the military should work in the family as well. How wrong he was!

In spite of his military ways, Dad could be a very compassionate and fun-loving husband and father. I have fond memories of lying on the floor with him for hours, playing with toy soldiers. In retrospect, I'm surprised Dad would even want to play war games, considering he had been up to his neck in combat a dozen years earlier.

In 1957 I first saw and heard an up-and-coming young star by the name of Elvis Presley. I went to the base theater and saw him star in a new movie called *Jail House Rock*. I went home and copied his moves in front of a mirror. Jan must have thought I had suffered a spastic attack from the way I danced around the room. Even though he had a goofy-sounding name, I thought this young guy with the jittery legs was pretty cool. I had no idea at the time that he would soon become an icon and a legend.

This was also the year when I learned to ride a bike. For Christmas, our parents bought Jan and me our first two-wheeled bicycles. It wasn't until thirty years later that Dad told me when he was a kid his family had been so poor he never had his own bike. I don't believe Mom did, either. My parents grew up during the Great Depression and didn't dream of having the things kids take for granted today. One of my fondest memories of my parents, is watching them riding around the neighborhood like a couple of excited kids on the brand-new bikes they bought each other for Christmas after they retired in McQueeney, Texas.

The summer of 1958, we moved to a nicer military housing complex, located between the Kelly Air Force Base flight line and Lackland Air Force Base. It was called The Cabbage Patch. Before the federal government bought the land that was eventually used to create Kelly Field in 1917, that part of San Antonio was covered in farmland, and cabbages were among the major crops. Although no one knew exactly where the name came from, the most logical explanation is that the housing complex replaced a large cabbage patch.

Comprised of an orderly, laid-out series of one-story quadplexes housing junior officers and their families, the community was a step up from the congested two-story apartments of Billy Mitchell Village. Not luxurious, but comfortable.

The complex was surrounded by tennis courts, a small park, a military depot, and a recreation building. Gleaming silver F-100 and F-102 fighter jets adorned the edge of the runway, the same runway where, in 1988, I saw the space shuttle Columbia arrive on the back of a Boeing 747. Jan and Mom hated the constant noise from the jets taking off and landing. I'm sure it scared Buddy a little, since he always walked around with his hands covering his ears, but to me it was heaven.

Spending hours with my fingers entwined in the chain link fence, captivated by this aeronautical playground, I dreamed about becoming a jet pilot when I grew up. When not staring at or daydreaming about flying the airplanes parked within a stone's throw of my front porch, I spent a lot of my spare time assembling models of those same planes.

Another fascinating feature of this neighborhood was living within a mile of one of the most amazing exhibits in the aviation world. Parked just off a road paralleling the runway was the XC-99, billed as the largest airplane in the world. It was an experimental cargo plane that had a two-story interior and sported six gigantic propellers mounted backwards on the wings. To me it looked like someone had turned the Empire State Building on it's side and added wheels and wings. The monstrous wheels were taller than our house.

The plane had been retired after ten years of service due to its fuel inefficiency, but not before it broke several long-distance hauling and load capacity records.

Now, it was relegated to being a tourist attraction. Years later, it was dismantled and shipped up north and reassembled as the feature exhibit in an Air Force aeronautical museum. In high school, I learned that the father of one of my friends was one of the original pilots.

During 1958 and 1959, Dad left the country on occasion without warning. As an intelligence officer and cryptologist, he spent a lot of time flying the borders of Communist China, Russia, and Korea, conducting electronic surveillance. Occasionally, his plane flew close to or over the borders and was tersely warned to back off or risk being shot down. He also flew into Vietnam in an advisory capacity years before our involvement in the Vietnam War. Mom wasn't thrilled with his absences, but Dad once told me he had the time of his life on those trips.

Years later, Dad described the one trip from which he almost didn't return. On September 2, 1958, he flew to Turkey to join up with a C-130 Hercules crew on a spy mission. Their assignment was to fly along the Soviet-Armenian border taking aerial photographs and gathering intelligence.

Dad arrived at the flight line in Turkey fifteen minutes past the scheduled time for the mission to depart. The officer in charge was a stickler for punctuality and refused to let him board the plane, even though it hadn't taxied to the runway yet. Dad begged him to reconsider, but the officer chose to be hardheaded and refused.

Dad had no choice but to return to his quarters and wait for the inevitable chewing-out he knew was coming from his commanding officer. The next day, he learned the plane had strayed over the Soviet Armenian border and had been shot down by four Russian fighter MiGs. He realized had he made the flight he would have been killed along with the rest of the crew.

In the 1970's, long after the Cold War had ended and the Russians had declassified many of their top secret files, someone in U.S. military intelligence sent Dad a picture. Taken by the pilot of one of the Russian MiGs, it showed, at close range, the doomed plane at the moment it blew up. Dad carried that picture in his wallet until the day he died and occasionally took it out and looked at it and thought about those brave souls who paid the ultimate price to protect our way of life.

During a trip to Japan, Dad bought me a brand-new trumpet. I didn't have the vaguest idea how to play it, but he, being so proficient (his words) on the French horn in high school, decided that instead of wasting money on lessons, I would learn the basics from him. He didn't teach me to read music, but he taught me my scales.

This gleaming creation of brass tubing and valves was the most beautiful thing I'd ever seen, and I was determined to master it. What intrigued me most was the tiny button on the bottom of the trumpet that was called the spit valve. I figured anything with the word spit in it had to be cool. Dad explained that, when being played, small amounts of saliva would accumulate at the bottom of the trumpet, and pressing the button would allow it to be blown out.

When my sister, Jan bragged about how great her violin was (she was in seventh grade and studying that instrument), I replied, "Yeah... but can you do this?" and then I grossed her out by chasing her around the house, showing her the projectile capabilities of a well-aimed spit valve.

When my music became too much for Mom to bear, she would usher me out the back door and encourage me to entertain the neighbors for a while. I'm sure the neighbors were real happy to see and hear me roaming the back alleys, belting out my rendition of "Has Anybody Seen my Gal?" I was actually pretty good, considering I never took a formal lesson.

One day, after having trouble learning a new song, I lost my temper and threw the trumpet down, denting it. When Dad saw it, he became so enraged he got a pair of pliers and broke the trumpet into little pieces. So much for my musical career. I think the neighbors were so relieved, they got together and sent him a thank-you note.

I liked to tail the base's DDT trucks cruising our neighborhood. They emitted clouds of smoke that were fun to hide in. I didn't realize that DDT was a toxic chemical used to kill mosquitoes and could cause *drain bamage* (a little pesticide humor).

Since Dad spent the majority of his time traveling overseas or golfing and Mom was busy taking care of Buddy, I was mostly unsupervised and still getting in more than my share of mischief. My best friend and I watched our next-door neighbors, who were being transferred, move their belongings out of their house. The next day, when we were sure they were finished and wouldn't be back, we decided to break in and see what their place looked like.

Instead of it being empty, we saw boxes of household items, sports equipment, and assorted toys. We thought it was generous of them to leave this cool stuff for the next tenants. Since we figured these things were abandoned, we snooped for anything worth taking or playing with. We found out later these things belonged to the people who were moving in.

We never did find anything worth taking, but we had a blast opening every package we could find. When we were done, there were linens, blankets, kitchen utensils, golf balls, and toys scattered all over the house. We totally wrecked the place, but we figured we would be long gone before anybody found out about it.

Before we left, I decided to wad up all the wrapping paper and stuff it into a big red wagon and set it on fire. I don't understand how I came up with that dumb idea. I struck a match and lit the paper, but it wasn't burning fast enough, so I leaned over and blew on the burning embers.

Suddenly the entire pile burst into flames. I jumped back but not before I realized my hair was on fire. I panicked and ran around the living room screaming that my head was on fire, while my friend was in hot pursuit (again, pun intended), smacking me in the head trying to put my hair out. He succeeded, but I must have looked a sight with my smoldering, spiky hair standing on end.

The noise and commotion must have alerted Mom, because within minutes she came charging through the door yelling, "What the hell is going on?"

After she put both fires out (miraculously, I was unhurt… for the moment), Mom made us help her clean up the mess. I don't know what she told our new neighbors, but since they were real nice to us, I figure she didn't spill the beans. However, they must have been scratching their heads in bewilderment, wondering who broke in and trashed their possessions, why was there a large black smudge on the ceiling, and most curious of all, what the deal was with the kid next door and that god-awful hair style.

One prank I pulled on my parents seemed clever at the time but could have jeopardized their health. While wandering through the field near my house, I came across an unusual pure white rock about the size of a baseball. It had a soft, porous surface, and when I rubbed my fingernail across it, a powdery residue with a texture like sugar came off in my hand. As I scraped off more of it, I got a brilliant idea. I ran home and wrapped it in a dish towel and pulverized it with a hammer. When I poured it into a bag, I knew my idea was going to work.

I went into the kitchen when Mom wasn't looking and grabbed the sugar bowl we kept on our kitchen table. I dumped the contents of the bowl into the container of sugar we kept in the pantry and replaced it with my fake sugar, and then waited in anticipation for supper. One of the staples at the dinner table was home-brewed tea. Mom and Dad loved to drink sweet tea and the rest of us usually drank milk.

When we finally sat for dinner, I eagerly waited for my parents nightly ritual. I barely disguised my glee when I saw Mom and Dad spooning the first portions of sugar into their tea. I watched intently as they finally took their first sips. They both got puzzled looks on their faces and added two more spoonfuls, Again, the puzzled looks. After a couple more spoonfuls, Dad stuck his finger in the sugar bowl and took a taste.

"Dot, where'd you get this sugar?" he asked.

"At the commissary," she answered.

"Well, what the hell's wrong with it? It doesn't even taste like sugar."

"How in the world do I know? I just bought it. I didn't make it."

"Well, goddammit, take it back and get a refund. And tell them they got a bad batch."

I could barely control my laughter, but I think from the furtive glances Jan shot me she must have suspected I had something to do with this. I could just imagine Mom returning the sugar and giving the manager hell for selling a defective product. The subject never came up again, but I'm sure Mom was too timid to complain to the commissary manager.

Mom, being the dutiful stay-at-home wife of an officer, volunteered some of her spare time for worthwhile causes. When I showed interest in becoming a Cub Scout, she offered to start a new Cub Scout pack and take on the responsibility of Den Mother. Having Mom as my Den Mother subjected me to some teasing from some of the other scouts, but she did a great job and made it fun.

I was eager to earn my Wolf and Bear achievement badges along with the silver and gold arrows, and she was very supportive. For one of my badges, Mom helped me make a golf scrapbook composed of articles I cut out of Dad's golf magazines. This stands out in my memory, because one of the articles I saved profiled an eighteen-year-old phenomenon who was predicted to take the golf world by storm some day. I remember seeing this picture of a husky-looking kid nicknamed "The Golden Boy." He grew up to be known as "The Golden Bear," more commonly known as Jack Nicklaus, the greatest golfer of all time.

For another badge, I needed to make a collection of something. I had no idea what to collect, until Mom suggested collecting unusual buttons. I dug through her sewing box and discovered several boxes of assorted buttons. I got a blank photo album and a bottle of glue and affixed all her buttons on the pages. There must have been hundreds of buttons.

When I showed it to Dad, he didn't seem too impressed. I didn't care, though. Mom thought it was the most beautiful button collection she'd ever seen—and I got my badge. Of course, the next time Mom needed to replace a button, I'm sure she wished I had collected butterflies or baseball cards instead.

For Christmas, Mom decided it would be a great idea to visit neighbors and ask them to donate used and broken toys to our Cub Scout pack. After collecting boxfuls of these items, we repaired and painted them, making the toys look as good as new. When we were done, we loaded them up into several cars. Our pack then climbed in and visited several specially-selected, low-income families in the Kelly Air Force Base area. I'll never forget the beaming smiles of these poor kids and the tears in the eyes of their appreciative parents (and Mom's tears, as well) when we showed up with all those shiny, new-looking toys. From the humble, dilapidated look of their houses, we realized these were probably the only Christmas presents they would receive that year.

Mom wasn't a very religious person, but she did teach Vacation Bible School during the summer of 1958. She studied the Bible enough to teach a classroom full of kids some of the more important Scriptures. I was very proud of Mom for taking the time to make others' lives better.

Despite Dad's frequent trips and obsession with golf, he did make time for us to do things together. He taught me to caddy and occasionally took me with him to either the old Kelly golf course or the Lackland golf course for his Saturday morning round with his buddies.

Electric carts had not been invented yet, so we had to use pull carts. Dad paid me a dollar a day plus hot dogs and cokes. He instructed me how to hand him the right club, as well as to keep my mouth shut and my eye on the ball. I think my most important lesson was to not let Mom know about all the four-letter words he liberally scattered around the course.

I learned a lot about golf and golf etiquette from Dad, but one of the most important things I learned one Saturday afternoon was *don't forget to wear shoes on the golf course*. I was used to running around the neighborhood bare-footed and just wasn't thinking. Dad would have reminded me if he'd noticed, but, unfortunately, he didn't. He still made me caddy the whole round like that. I found out that there are a lot of stickers on a golf course, so I can say I never made that mistake again. What a big distraction that must have been with my incessant exclamations of "Ouch! Oooh! Eeee!" every time I crossed a rough patch of stickers.

During the 1950's, kids didn't have the luxuries that they have today. Television was about ten years old, available only in black and white, and provided only three regular channels. About the only shows I watched were *Five Star Shock* every Friday night, featuring horror movies; *The Mickey Mouse Club* after school, which promoted the new Disneyland that had recently opened in Los Angeles; and the westerns *Have Gun Will Travel* and *Zorro* once a week. I loved *Zorro* so much that my parents bought me a Zorro outfit for Christmas. I ran around The Cabbage Patch with my black hat, mask, and gloves cracking my trusty whip at every dog and cat that crossed my path.

In those days, my friends and I spent most of our time outdoors playing marbles, mumblety-peg (a dangerous game played with pocketknives), and cowboys and Indians. We also enjoyed building forts out of scrap lumber and cardboard boxes. Few things surpass the active imaginations of a bunch of nine-year-old boys. Dad told lots of stories about the "good old days." I didn't realize it at the time, but I was creating some pretty memorable "good old days" myself.

One weekend, our parents took us to Nuevo Laredo for sightseeing and shopping. It was my first trip to Mexico, and I was surprised at how run-down and dirty the town was. The only souvenirs I remember getting were a pair of colorful maracas and a genuine leather bull whip (better than the one that came with the Zorro outfit). The maracas lasted a long time, but the bullwhip only lasted one week.

The next Friday night, Jim and Flora Borden (my parents' best friends) came to visit and brought their kids, Jeanne and Nancy. For some reason, I got mad at Jeanne. She was the same age as Jan and, as usual, they were picking on me. Too afraid of Jan, I figured I could handle Jeanne, so I grabbed my bullwhip and went after her. I popped her pretty good with it, and all hell broke loose. She screamed, and that got our parents' attention. When Dad found out what I had done, he got a knife and chopped my bullwhip into little pieces. First my trumpet and now my bullwhip. He sure had a knack for taking things apart.

After Christmas, Grandpa and Grandma Frier drove from Winter Haven, Florida to visit us. It snowed while they were here, which really surprised them since they didn't think it snowed in Texas. The highlight of that trip was when Grandpa told me he got a job at Dairy Queen. To a kid, that was the perfect job… I mean, they sell ice cream there. I couldn't wait to tell my friends at school how important Grandpa was.

On one of his trips to Germany, Dad bought me a souvenir that has to be the worst I ever received. It was a pair of lederhosen: green leather shorts with suspenders that had ivory carvings of deer on the front. They were popular among the Germans. Ugliest thing I ever saw. He made me model them for his guests at his incessant cocktail parties. Why couldn't he have brought me something cool like a Luger pistol or swastika-engraved bayonet? I think I burned those lederhosen during his next trip overseas.

After living in The Cabbage Patch for a year, it was time for the Willis vagabonds to move. Our destination: Wallingford, Connecticut. Dad was going to attend Yale University's foreign language school full-time for one year to master the Korean language in preparation for his next duty station: Korea. He said we all might be able to go overseas with him. I had no idea where Connecticut was until Mom showed me on the map. When she told me it snowed in Connecticut, I couldn't wait to get there.

I loved living in The Cabbage Patch. I drove by there in the 1970's and it was gone—replaced by a park and a softball field. Fond memories came flooding back from those days. What a great time and place to be a kid!

Four

A Dinner Tale

In the summer of 1934, the New York Yankees visited Norfolk, Virginia, to play their farm league team, the Norfolk Tars, in an exhibition game. The Yankees barely won the game, by a score of eleven to nine. This Yankee team included baseball greats Babe Ruth, Lou Gehrig, and Bill Dickey.

This was the infamous game in which Lou Gehrig took a fastball to the head, a ball thrown by Tar's pitcher, Ray White, in the second inning. Gehrig, known as "The Iron Horse," was knocked unconscious for a few minutes and had to leave the game. In those days, batting helmets had not yet been introduced. Despite having a broken toe and knot on his head the size of an egg, Gehrig played the Washington Senators the next day against doctor's orders. There has been much speculation over the years that this concussion might have been instrumental in Gehrig's bout with, and ultimate death from, amyotrophic lateral sclerosis (ALS), now referred to as Lou Gehrig's Disease.

What is so significant about this particular game other than Lou Gehrig's beaning? In attendance that day was an eleven-year-old boy by the name of Buddy, more formally known as Sidney Willis, and he wasn't just sitting in the stands with the other spectators—he was sitting in the Yankees' dugout with Ruth, Gehrig, Dickey, and the rest of the Bronx Bombers, as they were endearingly called by their fans.

Does this sound a little far-fetched? According to Dad, he bought a ticket with his friends like everyone else. Before the game started, however, the announcer told the spectators to carefully check the numbers on their ticket stubs, because six numbers were going to be called at random. The lucky holders of these tickets were not only going to be escorted to the Yankees dugout to receive a baseball autographed by the entire team, they were also going to be allowed to sit in the dugout with the players, giving them a ringside seat to the game.

Being a Yankees fan, Dad was thrilled. After the game, he took the ball home and stashed it in his dresser drawer. If Granddad had any idea of the value of that autographed baseball, he would have locked it away in a safe place.

In 1934, the depression was hitting everyone hard, especially the Willis family. Luxuries like baseballs were hard to come by, so when the beat-up baseball Dad and his friends were using became mangled beyond repair (in those days, ripped and torn leather covers were taped over repeatedly until there was nothing left to tape), he retrieved that souvenir ball from its hiding place and took it outside to meet its fate.

Dad and his friends were too young and poor at the time to realize what a tragedy that was. The fate of that ball followed that of all the other sandlot baseballs before

it—beaten and battered until it became an unrecogniz-
able mass of horsehide, string, cork, and tape, the faded
and hallowed autographs but a distant memory of a by-
gone era.

We hit the road after I finished school. It took several days to get there, and I was mesmerized when we drove through New York City—I had never seen skyscrapers before. Dad pointed out the Empire State Building, at the time the tallest building in the world. I knew of this building because it was the same one King Kong had climbed in the movie. At 102 stories, it towered over the skyline. Jan and I wanted to go up in it, but Dad said we would have to do it another time.

As we crossed the border into Connecticut, a different world unfolded. I had never seen so much green foliage and such beautiful trees. San Antonio, by comparison, was dusty, rocky, and brown. It had its own intrinsic beauty, but this was different.

Dad told us that the seasonal changes in New England were much more pronounced and colorful than they are in Texas, as we would soon discover. While living in Connecticut, we would be fortunate enough to watch the trees turn into an explosion of color and see the winter snows transform the landscape into an amazing wonderland, as beautiful as any Norman Rockwell painting.

A whole new panorama of color greeted us in springtime when the flowers bloomed. And the summer! We weren't confronted with varying shades of brown and oppressive heat, as was the norm in the south Texas summers. I've traveled to many places in my lifetime, and nothing compares to the beauty of the seasonal changes in New England.

When we arrived in Wallingford, a small town seven miles north of New Haven, I was surprised by the different elevations. San Antonio lies on a flat plain south of the Texas Hill Country. That flat, monotonous landscape is occasionally punctuated by slight rises that some locals refer to as hills, but, compared to what I was now witnessing, they seemed like nothing more than mole hills. Here, roads and streets curved up and down and around an infinite number of rolling green hills. The only drawback was that I don't think I spied a single suitable plot of ground flat enough on which to play a decent game of baseball (my new passion).

It didn't take long for us to locate our house, with which I instantly fell in love. It was a small, one-story, three-bedroom house with a carport. To me, however, it was a mansion, a castle transported smack dab into the middle of a kid's paradise. I could actually walk around it: it wasn't attached to other homes like the duplexes, quadplexes, and apartments I had lived in for the past nine years.

Our house was in a small community on a dead-end street. There were no fences in sight—people trusted each other more in those days. Beyond the back yard was a huge crop field sloping gently up-hill for half a mile. On the other side of this field was Cooke State Park, easily within walking distance.

Down to the right, our neighbors' back yard opened up to a perfectly rectangular shaped forest, covering about five acres.

This forest was bordered by a spacious meadow with a steep incline that provided excellent sledding during the winter. Behind the forest was an apple orchard and a big pond surrounded by cattails, which was used as an ice-skating rink in the winter and a fishing hole the rest of the year. I always found interesting things to do back there and spent countless hours collecting tadpoles and frogs from the pond, eating green apples until I got sick, or collecting kindling wood from the forest for our fireplace. The rest of Wallingford consisted of an endless succession of fields, meadows, and forests. Since I was only nine, Mom didn't allow me to explore as far afield as I would have liked.

This was the first time I wished Dad would quit the Air Force. I wanted to spend the rest of my life here. Crossing the street and standing in our neighbor's back yard, I could almost see the entire town spread out below.

From that neighbor's yard, I sometimes sat patiently on the hillside and waited for Dad to come home from his classes at Yale. I would first catch a glimpse of his car rounding a bend in the road, then anxiously watch it meander through a series of turns as it slowly progressed up the hill. It would finally make a tight right turn and zoom up the very steep Rock Hill Road to our street. I say *zoom* because the hill was so steep Dad had to gun the engine to pick up enough speed to make it. When the road iced up in the winter, he had to either put snow chains on his tires or wait for the city road crews to salt the roads.

Rock Hill Elementary School was close by, so I walked home from school for lunch. While eating my peanut butter and jelly sandwich and tomato soup, I watched re-runs of "The Restless Gun" on our black-and-white television.

Since I enjoyed being a Cub Scout in San Antonio, I asked Mom to sign me up with the local pack. Although she was too busy to be a den mother again, she supported me one hundred percent, taking me to all the meetings and outings.

My favorite scouting event was the annual pine-wood derby, where we raced small cars carved out of blocks of pine. The racing car kits came with wheels and axles that were standard, but we were able to express our individuality in the shape of the car. Dad taught me how to carve the wood without stabbing myself, then guided me through the sandpapering and painting process. This was our first father and son woodworking project, and we enjoyed it immensely.

The night of the big race, my car competed admirably with all the others. Since we were allowed to use our imagination in our designs, there was quite a variety of shapes and colors. Some sported beautiful, professional-looking paint jobs (I'm sure the fathers of those boys contributed a little more than they should have) and others looked like the original blocks of wood with a minimum amount of paint splattered on them (these kids were probably on their own). Some cars even lost their wheels on the way down the track (their dads were probably accountants or writers).

Dad was a great help and encouraged me to come up with my own design. My car didn't win, but he and I still felt like winners. The quality time we spent together made the experience worthwhile. For the rest of his life, Dad and I both enjoyed working on various wood projects, some together and some individually.

I believed in the positive aspects of scouting so much that, years later, as a Coast Guard Academy cadet, I did volunteer work with the New London, Connecticut Boy Scout Troop. I didn't get to help carve any race cars, but I did have a blast teaching Boy Scouts how to use Morse Code.

Friends and I built our own baseball field, stretching across several back yards. It wasn't easy playing baseball on the side of a hill, but we had a great time. The father of one of my friends built a backstop behind the home plate out of wooden poles and canvas. We meticulously scraped dirt together and made a professional-looking pitcher's mound. Our mothers fabricated bags for bases. We talked our parents into buying us matching red shirts so we would look like a real team.

Back then, no one had heard of Little League baseball. During the two summers I lived there, we played two games a day. We played one game in the morning, went home for lunch, then returned for another game in the afternoon. Not an adult in sight—just the way sandlot baseball was meant to be played.

Modern Little League baseball, while it has some merit, has too much parental influence. Give the kids bats, balls, gloves, and access to a vacant lot, and then get the heck out of their way. Let them figure the game out for themselves, have some fun, and go home when it's dark. In those days, we learned how to play baseball, how to get along with others, and how to fight and settle our differences without the interference of parents. We could use more of that philosophy today.

When not playing baseball, I was watching it on television with Dad. If one of us left the room, the other would have to give a complete update upon our return. He had been a die-hard Yankees fan from childhood, and I was becoming one as well. Dad claimed to be a pretty good baseball player while growing up and encouraged me in my quest to master the game.

For some reason, he wanted me to become a catcher, so he bought me a new catcher's mitt and mask. I was probably the only kid in town with catcher's equipment. We spent countless hours in the yard where he pitched me high fly balls, grounders, knuckleballs, and fastballs. He also taught me how to trust my mask and not flinch when a batter swung the bat in front of my face. I think he was living out his baseball dreams vicariously through me.

Dad's lessons must have worked, because, after joining a youth league two years later, I was asked to catch. Fortunately, my catching skills made up for lack of hitting and base running skills. To this day, visiting a sporting goods store wouldn't be complete without my stopping by the baseball gloves and sniffing their intoxicating leather aroma, which never fails to transport me back to those warm afternoons when my father was teaching me the rudiments of America's favorite pastime.

Dad took me fishing for the first time while we lived in Connecticut. Before going, we went to the pond beyond the apple orchard, where he showed me how to rake the leaves along the bank to find insects to use for bait. We then went to the expansive lawn of Choate Preparatory School near New Haven (where John F. Kennedy was schooled) at night and looked for nightcrawlers. After we collected enough bait, we went to a nearby lake where we caught a stringer of bluegills. Even though I never cared much for fish as a kid, the ones we caught and Mom fried up for dinner were the best-tasting fish I ever had.

I was selected to be a Wise Man in our school Christmas play. Mom bought me a robe for my costume. This was my second experience with show business. I had no lines but felt pretty important standing on the stage before a packed auditorium. I have such a sentimental attachment to the robe Mom helped me pick out that I've kept it in a special compartment in my closet for the past fifty-three years. I occasionally caress the worn fabric between my fingers and think about her.

Since television had not yet permeated every aspect of our lives, my sister, Jan, and I spent a lot of time together. We received a weekly allowance of one dollar each, and every Saturday afternoon (after watching cartoons, of course) we took our meager allotment and headed down Rock Hill Road to a small store, where we spent it all on penny candy. Yes, you could actually buy candy for a penny in those days.

Another activity that Jan dreamed up was our occasional talent show. Jan was creative and recruited me to help her put on these shows for the neighborhood kids. Acting should have been my career, because I thoroughly enjoyed performing. To this day, I'm still a bit of a ham—I'm sure my friends and family would agree with this.

We put on a short play or skit one week and the next week performed a musical. Jan made up the material, song lyrics, and dance routines, and I did pretty much whatever she told me to do. She was the leader and I the follower. We put a lot of effort and planning into our productions. I remember turning off the ceiling lights and making spotlights out of lampshades that were strategically laid on their sides. For one of the musical revues, I put on a borrowed top hat, held a cane, and did a very impressive soft-shoe routine for the audience.

When the snows came, the Willis kids had a blast. We sledded and tobogganed. We wanted to learn to ice-skate but couldn't afford the skates. I remember the snow being three feet deep in our yard, deep enough for short tunnels. I saw twelve-foot snow drifts touching the eaves of our house. We even built a good-sized igloo in one of the snow drifts.

The long sloping hills made for great sledding. While I was preparing to sled down a particularly steep slope, Buddy asked to ride with me. Being a good big brother, I said, "No. Get lost."

While I was climbing to the top of the hill, he waited nonchalantly off to the side about halfway down the slope. As I zoomed by him, he suddenly lunged at me and landed diagonally on my back. I quickly lost control with the added weight and started zigzagging off course. We ended up crashing head first into a huge boulder, hitting it so hard that we went flying through the air, landing in a snow drift. We weren't seriously hurt, but we were so shook up we went home bawling.

That year, we celebrated our first white Christmas since we'd left Illinois. I remember strolling through the forest near our house with Jan and Buddy on Christmas Eve. The light of a full moon reflected off the new fallen snow, and it was so quiet and serene one could have heard a pin drop.

We were bundled up against the cold brisk air and were gathering kindling for our Christmas fire. Buddy and I still believed in Santa Claus and we kept a sharp lookout for an early arrival of his sleigh and reindeer. The snow was untouched except for our footprints and even our whispers seemed to carry for miles. Jan didn't believe in Santa anymore, but she did search the cloudless sky for the Christmas star.

After loading up as much wood as we could carry, we trudged home through the magical white powder. Once we discarded our heavy coats, gloves, boots, and scarves, Mom rewarded us with homemade snow cream: a rare treat made from fresh snow, sugar, and vanilla. Staring at our beautifully decorated Christmas tree, I silently made another wish that Santa wouldn't forget to bring me the Fanner-Fifty cap pistol I had asked him for.

Dad spent weekdays in class at Yale and studied for hours at the dinner table in the evening. He had a tape recorder with headphones, and would endlessly recite his Korean lessons. It sounded like gibberish to me, but Dad caught on to it real fast, since he had already spent time in Korea and was familiar with the language. By the end of the year, he spoke fluent Korean.

In the spring of 1960, our parents took us to Manhattan to visit Mom's Uncle Bob. He was Grandpa's brother, whom I had never met, and lived in one of the upper floors of a high-rise building. While our parents were talking to Uncle Bob, Jan and I were leaning out of the living room window staring in fascination at the busy street below. We spent the entire time trying to see how many pedestrians we could spit on. Every now and then we would get a bulls-eye and smile and wave as they looked up and shook their fists at us. It was a good thing Buddy was too little to participate. Knowing him, he would have probably dropped rocks on their heads instead.

We finally convinced Dad to take us up in the Empire State Building. It was an amazing feeling being that high up. We could see the whole city spread out below.

Being a very sociable person, Dad hosted a backyard barbeque for his Korean instructors. To reinforce their Korean language lessons, they insisted that it was important for Dad and them to converse in Korean. That was well and good for them, but the rest of our family felt left out listening to them jabbering away in this strange-sounding language. Dad told me years later he and Mom almost adopted a Korean orphan boy when he was stationed in Korea in 1956. If he had, I might have already learned the language from my new brother and fit right in with the Korean instructors.

One of the instructors brought his cute ten-year-old daughter. We didn't share a common language, but I was smitten, and being the showoff that I was, I decided to impress her with my daring acrobatic skills. After catching her eye, I gave her a sly smile and lifted a plastic lawn chair onto the picnic table. I climbed up, sat in the chair, and leaned back, balancing on the chair's back legs. She giggled. Emboldened, I flashed her my best performer's smile and stuck my arms and legs out. Acting was my forte, but my balancing skills weren't quite up to snuff. After a couple of seconds, I flipped over backwards, bounced off the table, and landed on my head.

Nobody saw this act of lunacy except the girl, who, by now, was no longer giggling—she was laughing hysterically. Humiliated, I ran into the house and hid, refusing to come out until I was sure she had gone home.

My friends and I decided we were going to build a high jump to prepare us to become track stars. We made it out of two-by-fours, nails, and a broomstick.

After a while, Dad came out and watched us. Suffering under the delusion that he was the world's leading expert on every subject under the sun, Dad decided to show us how it was done. I don't think he ever participated in a track event in his life, but that didn't stop him from lecturing us on the physics and proper technique of high jumping.

After telling us we had it all wrong, Dad decided to show us his special technique. He backed up, hesitated a few seconds, and took off, high-stepping like the experts did. This expertise ended, however, when he went sailing over the bar. I guess Dad hadn't had time to perfect his landing, because as soon as he left the ground his arms and legs didn't seem to want to cooperate with each other. He landed with a thud on his side and started screaming in agony.

When Mom came out to see what all the commotion was all about, Dad yelled, "Dot, take me to the emergency room! I think I broke something."

Mom eased him into the car, muttering something to the effect, "Idiot. Moron. You damn fool, are you trying to get yourself killed?"

We thought it was pretty funny and continued with our practicing. I found out later that Dad had cracked his collarbone. After that, he left us alone in our Olympic aspirations.

Every spring, a farmer plowed and tilled the field behind our house. Between crop harvests, an abundance of wild strawberry vines took over the field. I've never had strawberries as tasty as those. I have fond memories of strolling through those patches with Jan, gathering buckets full of those sweet berries.

One day, my best friend and I noticed the farmer driving a tractor that was pulling a funny-looking contraption behind it. It had spinning blades that were flinging dirt clods in its wake. We decided it would be fun to run along behind the tractor and see if we could dodge these missiles. Kind of like a game of machine gun dodge ball.

The farmer didn't seem to mind us trailing behind him—in fact, he seemed amused by our antics. After being plastered by these bombs, it didn't take long for us to realize that these weren't dirt clods: they were clumps of cow manure, used to fertilize the crops. By the time we made this crappy observation, it was too late—we stunk to high heaven.

Our moms weren't too thrilled when we got home, but I guess it was safer than running through smoke clouds emitted by DDT trucks in The Cabbage Patch the year before. Inhaling manure odors wasn't quite as dangerous as ingesting toxic pesticides.

When the summer of 1960 came to a close, we were told it was time to move again. Leaving this paradise was painful, but I knew by then that the life of a military brat involved regularly pulling up stakes and moving on to new adventures.

Dad told us that our next move was going to take us out of the country. Instead of being sent to Korea, he was being assigned to a two-year tour of duty in Okinawa, a Japanese island, about three hundred miles south of the mainland. *An island? Wow, how cool is that?* I thought. I couldn't wait to get there. As it turned out, Dad had to report right away, but the rest of us were going to have to move to Winter Haven, Florida and find a temporary place to live near Mom's parents.

I was told that our departure for Okinawa would be delayed six months or longer for two reasons: We had to get on a waiting list for family military housing, and we had to undergo a long series of immunization shots, preparing us for life abroad. Shots again? Jan and I weren't too happy with that news. I still had bad memories of all those childhood shots we had endured several years earlier.

We were moving to Winter Haven so Mom's parents could help her with the kids. I soon discovered that the time we spent there would provide some of my grandest memories.

Five

A Dinner Tale

In 1920, a twenty-four-year-old woman left the family farm, located a mile outside of Twin City, Georgia, to look for work in Savannah. The tenth of sixteen children, Minda Mae Neal, my maternal grandmother, found a job in a tobacco factory, rolling and packing cigars, and rented a room in a boarding house. A year later she married a handsome young man named William Frier, and over the next nine years they had five children.

William was born first, and four daughters — Blanche, Christine, Doris (my mother), and Helen — were born within seven years.

Grandpa worked in a foundry molding train wheels. He and Grandma made enough money to buy a house and a car, and his family enjoyed all the comforts of the middle class. Then in 1929, everything fell apart. The Great Depression hit, and Grandpa lost his job. My grandparents also lost their house and most of their savings.

Another train wheel foundry job became available in Portsmouth, Virginia, so Grandpa moved the family there, getting a ride on a school bus, driven by one of Grandma's brothers. Her brother "borrowed" the bus *from his employer on a Saturday morning and delivered the Frier family to Virginia late that night. He returned to Savannah on Sunday in time to drive kids to school on Monday.*

The foundry business was slack and, though steady, only provided Grandpa with employment two or three days a week. Since that barely covered the grocery bill of around twelve dollars a week, my grandparents brought in a little extra money by taking in a boarder for a few years. During that time, all five kids shared one bed-room.

Money was still scarce, and Christmas presents usually consisted of shoes and clothes (some made by Grandma). The kids played outside barefoot to save their shoes for school and church. In those tough times, it wasn't unusual for holes in shoes to be covered by cardboard.

In the late 1930's, when the economy began to im-prove, the Friers' financial situation was on the up-swing as well, and they were finally able to buy another second-hand car to replace the one they lost in the Great Depression.

We drove to Florida just before school started. Goodbye, land of crisp, intoxicating colors. Hello, land of beautiful, warm sunshine. What a difference there was between Connecticut and Florida. Winter Haven was a small town similar in size to Walling-ford, but flat and sandy and filled with lakes. It didn't take me long to push to the back of my mind those incredible memories of that paradise in Connecticut.

Instead of apple orchards, wild strawberry fields, and cattail-encircled ponds, I was now surrounded by orange, grapefruit, and tangerine trees, lakes, and alligators.

Alligators? Up until then, I thought you would have to visit the zoo to see these creatures, but according to Grandpa Frier, the lakes in Florida were infested with them. I thought he was pulling my leg until he pointed out the eyes of a three-footer lounging in the shallows of Lake Silver. I found out it was fairly safe to swim in the lakes as long as I kept my eyes open (and my legs moving).

Dad got us settled in a rental house near the Friers, then left for Okinawa. He would send for us as soon as housing became available. It didn't make any difference to me whether we went to Korea or Okinawa—I was excited about the thought of living in a foreign country. Dad said we should be ready to leave for Okinawa around February, 1961.

I still remember the glee with which Grandpa drove us, wide-eyed and apprehensive, to the dispensary for our shots. I loved Grandpa, and I know he loved us, but he seemed to get a kick out of our fear of shots.

Winter Haven is in central Florida, midway between Tampa and Orlando. I had never seen so many lakes in my life, and they all seemed to be interconnected by short bridges.

Citrus groves dotted the landscape as well. I couldn't walk three blocks in any direction without running into a grove of orange, grapefruit, or tangerine trees. It wasn't uncommon to see these trees in people's yards, as well. My grandparents' back yard had a lime tree and a kumquat tree.

On my last visit to Winter Haven, I noticed these groves are now fenced in to keep outsiders from taking the fruit. Back then, the groves were open to the public.

Jan and I made many a trip to the groves, lugging large cardboard boxes, to pick as much free fruit as we could carry back to our house and our grandparents' house.

Times sure have changed.

The town was small enough that Jan and I could walk to school, downtown, or anywhere else we needed to go. Even though we lived there only eight months, I learned my way around and had a lot of fun and made a bunch of friends.

My grandparents loved to fish, but preferred to do it the old-fashioned way: using a cane pole with a short line, a float, and a single hook with a worm as bait. Tom Sawyer and Huckleberry Finn would have fit right in with those two. I spent many happy and peaceful hours with them, fishing from several of the numerous small bridges. We would dangle our feet over the edge, wondering what whoppers we were going to catch that day (and I was secretly wondering what gators were going to catch us).

One of our favorite places that Grandpa took Buddy and me that year, and on other visits years later, was Sand Mountain. It was a huge pile of sand about one hundred feet high that had some industrial use. It wasn't locked behind a fence, so Grandpa figured it must be okay for us to use it. Buddy and I repeatedly trudged up to the top and then ran full-speed down to the bottom, crashing into each other, doing flips and flops, and flinging our bodies every way imaginable.

Grandpa never rushed us—he just sat on the hood of his light blue sedan with his arms crossed and a big grin on his face. I think he may have been having more fun than we were. When we were spent and couldn't climb another step, he would open the car door, tell us to shake the sand out of our clothes, load us up and take us home. Of course, Grandma would raise holy hell when we walked in the front door of their house, flinging sand everywhere.

I mentioned earlier that Grandpa was a retired train wheel factory foreman. He received a small pension, but sometimes worked at odd jobs to make a little extra money. One of his neighbors owned a Dairy Queen and hired Grandpa to sweep the parking lot on occasion. It seems like a menial job now, but at the time I thought any job at Dairy Queen was cool and really important, especially when he would let me tag along, and the boss let us eat all the free ice cream we wanted.

Grandpa always took me with him, because he knew that in a few months we would be gone, and who knew when we would see each other again. He also realized that with Dad overseas, I needed him to be there as a sort of father figure. I sat patiently on the curb and watched this sixty-two-year-old man pushing a broom around the parking lot. If he was embarrassed at all, he didn't show it—he would occasionally look over in my direction and give me a big smile and a wave.

He was a proud man, but not too proud to have his grandson watch him do whatever it took to help put food on his table. I didn't realize it at the time, but I now know that he was the perfect embodiment of what a real family man should be.

Another job Grandpa took was lawn mowing. I helped him unload the lawn mower from the car and, once again, took up my position on the curb. I stared in awe at him, thinking that he must be awfully important to be entrusted with taking care of other people's yards. When he finished, I helped him load the mower into the car, and we headed home.

When Dad came home on a short leave, he and I went fishing with Grandpa at one of the local lakes. For some reason, instead of getting to fish, I was given the dubious honor of retrieving snagged hooks. They used cane poles, and the shoreline was full of reeds that kept grabbing their hooks.

"You're up, Bill," they would say, and off I'd go, wading neck deep into that snake- and gator-infested water to unsnag the hook. I felt like a Labrador retriever. I'm surprised they didn't toss me a biscuit when I waded ashore.

Despite my tenure as man's best friend, I enjoyed the sights, sounds, and smells of the lake. Spanish moss covered the cypress trees along the shoreline like giant shrouds, their grey spongy tentacles nearly touching the ground. A soft morning rain dampened the moss enough that it gave off a tangy, musty smell that lingered in the air for hours.

The mud banks were home to all sorts of creatures including frogs, lizards, snakes and the occasional alligator. The incessant buzzing of insects was a distraction at first but eventually receded into the tranquility and peacefulness of the afternoon.

That day, the mosquitoes were out in force, so Dad told me to gather up a huge pile of Spanish moss. We lit it, and it made an impressive bonfire. The smoke deterred the mosquitoes, but was so thick and acrid that we almost choked to death.

Despite those humble conditions, I enjoyed myself, savoring those rare moments with Dad and Grandpa. We teased each other and talked about anything and everything. Watching the camaraderie between Dad and Grandpa left me with a warm feeling inside. Despite their differences in age and background, they seemed to enjoy each other's company immensely. I wanted that day to last forever. In fact, if they were both alive right now, and we got to go fishing one last time, and I got to hear those magic words, "You're up, Bill," I would just smile and say, "Get it yourself, you lazy bums! I'm retired."

My first experience with racism occurred during my stay in Winter Haven. One of my new friends was a white kid from a migrant family that circulated around the country harvesting seasonal crops. I had read about migrant families in John Steinbeck's *The Grapes of Wrath* but had no idea they still existed. At that time, his family was picking fruit in the citrus groves in central Florida. He said it was the only life he knew.

My friend's family exhibited strong white-supremacist views. I was naive and didn't understand the slurs they used and wasn't too concerned, until a sad event opened my eyes.

One day, my friend invited me to accompany him and a bunch of his other buddies to "walk the niggers" from Lake Silver. I had no idea what he was talking about. He explained that they were going to walk the beach, brandishing sticks and chains, and evict these unwelcome people from the lake. Resistance usually resulted in beatings. I was appalled and told him I wanted no part of this. If I had any guts, I would have shown up in support of the blacks, but I'm sure I would have taken a beating as well. I was only ten, but I was rapidly learning the ways of the world and wasn't too pleased with some of the things I saw.

My best friend's dad was a Baptist preacher and was always trying to get Jan and me to attend his sermons. I had heard that Baptist services were loud and boisterous, so, out of curiosity, I talked Jan into going with me one Sunday.

That son-of-a-bitch preacher zeroed in on us right away as we sat quietly in the front pew. He went on and on about how my sister and I needed to be "saved" in order to get into heaven. He got the whole congregation riled up into saving these poor children, and before long one of them took Jan's hand and pulled her up on stage next to the pulpit. By now, Jan was crying and I was terrified. Soon, I was pulled up there as well, after which the preacher and his fanatical followers threw their hands in the air and announced we were saved. Jan and I got out of there as soon as we could.

When we told Mom about this, she was furious and didn't want us going anywhere near there again. Good thing Dad was overseas. There's no telling what he would have done to that preacher. This experience had a lot to do with Jan's and my ambivalence towards organized religion.

While in the fifth grade at Brigham Elementary, I got another stab at show business. Our class was putting on a play about the circus, and I had volunteered to work with the set decorators. Most of the acting parts would be kids dressed as various circus animals.

One day, our class was gathered around a piano during our music appreciation time. As we were singing away, my teacher pulled me aside and told me I had a nice singing voice. She was the play's musical director, and she told me she wanted me to sing a solo for the play. I had no idea what it was about, but since it had a circus theme, I was interested. I figured that since I had such an extensive circus performing background (my horseback riding debacle three years previously), I would be a natural.

She handed me the lyrics to "The Daring Young Man on the Flying Trapeze" and told me to try singing it while she accompanied me on the piano. I must admit, my voice sounded pretty good. When she told

71

me I needed to practice in front of a live audience, I was a little apprehensive. Singing in a group in class was one thing, but singing solo in front of a crowd was something else.

She talked me into getting up on stage and practicing in front of the other cast members and set decorators. After a few attempts, I became more comfortable—I even did it a cappella a few times. Suddenly, I was a big shot. Even the cute girls started noticing me. *I could see doing this as a career*, I thought to myself. I even started throwing in a couple of well-placed, operatic hand flourishes to impress my legions of fans.

Two weeks before the performance, the teacher called me up to her desk during class. She handed me a bag containing my costume and told me to go to the boys' room and try it on for size. She told one of the other boys to accompany me to guard the door while I tried it on. *Oh boy! It's probably a cool top hat with a black coat with tails like the circus ringmasters wear in the movies*, I was thinking. Instead, I pulled out a red tank top and a pair of skimpy red leotards. *What the hell?*

There was nothing else in the bag, so I tried them on. About that time, the other boy walked in, took one look at me and collapsed to the floor in convulsive laughter. I looked down and realized that the thin material didn't do a very good job of concealing certain parts of my body. I would have beaten the crap out of him for laughing, except I knew it wouldn't bode too well for me to be seen visiting the principal's office in that get-up.

"Son of a bitch!" I yelled and immediately changed back into my other clothes. I stormed back into the classroom and tossed the bag onto my teacher's desk.

"I can't wear this," I said. "Where's my top hat and coat?"

She informed me that I was a trapeze artist, not a ringmaster, and this is what trapeze artists wear. I still refused to wear it, but she wouldn't budge. She told me I had two choices: wear the outfit or go back with the set decorators. I chose the latter.

When the play opened, I was backstage admiring my artwork on the tent stripes, but occasionally, I shot an envious—if not murderous—look at the pansy who had stolen my spotlight. *The dramatic world hasn't heard the last of me*, I thought bitterly.

Six

A Dinner Tale

In the fall of 1944, General Douglas MacArthur led American and Filipino soldiers in the Battle of Leyte Island in the Philippines, one of the major battles of World War II.

The goal of this campaign was to end the three-year occupation by the Imperial Japanese Army and help bring the war in the Pacific to an end.

The United States Army's 96th Division was with the first regiment that landed on Leyte Island. Mom's older brother, William Frier, a twenty-one-year-old private first class, served in that division. He was a long way from his home in Portsmouth, Virginia, and was probably wondering what the hell he was doing in this God-forsaken place halfway around the world.

On the second night, a Japanese mortar barrage killed one soldier and wounded two others, one of whom was Uncle William.

Since a hospital had not been set up, they were returned to their ship. The other soldier died aboard ship and was buried at sea. According to Uncle William, that was a very touching moment. His shoulder wound kept him out of action for a month.

In the spring of 1945, Uncle William's reserve unit landed on the island of Okinawa and participated in another major battle of the war. He was involved in serious fighting at the Shuri Castle line on the southern half of the island. During the fight, he scrambled through unsecured areas to deliver a message to headquarters, an action for which he was awarded the Bronze Star. He was wounded a second time several days later but returned to action the next day. He was also awarded two Purple Hearts (on which his name was engraved) for wounds received in action.

The Battle of Okinawa lasted eighty-two days. Several months later, after the historic atomic bombings of Hiroshima and Nagasaki, Japan surrendered. Those two battles in which Uncle William participated did much to bring the Japanese Empire to its knees. Our country owes its thanks to this man for his sacrifice and service to our country.

On February 6, 1961, we got the call to come to Okinawa. I enjoyed living in Florida but was excited about moving overseas. Unfortunately, Granddad Willis's death on January 24 had put us in a somber mood. I still had fond memories of our short time together watching television and hanging around the barbershop.

I recall sitting on the floor of their living room in the evening, next to Granddad's easy chair, watching a new TV western called *Gunsmoke*. Granddad lived for that show. When I watch re-runs of *Gunsmoke* today, I can almost smell the bitter aroma of the block of tobacco he incessantly carved chunks out of with his pocket knife and popped into his mouth. The gunshots on the show were often punctuated with spurts of tobacco juice flying from Granddad's pursed lips as he expertly zinged the empty coffee can resting on the floor between us. I think I got "hit" as much as the desperados Matt Dillon was casually outdrawing. I could have moved, but I enjoyed sitting next to Granddad and figured the occasional tobacco stain was worth it.

Other than those special occasions and the times I spent sitting on the bench, watching him cut hair, Granddad and I didn't do much together. He was a quiet, stern man who kept to himself. He died when I was ten, so I never had the chance to get to know him as well as I got to know my other grandparents.

When it was time for us to go to Okinawa, Grandpa Frier dropped us off at the Tampa airport where we had a long series of flights ahead of us. We flew to Dallas, then on to Los Angeles, followed by a short hop to Seattle, where we spent the night. In the morning we flew to Anchorage, Alaska.

After a three-hour wait in the terminal, we boarded for our long, tedious flight to Tokyo.

The flight across the Pacific took nine hours. I was sick the entire time, and Mom was having a miserable time as well. Mom and Buddy sat in the front section of the plane, their seats directly behind two seats that were positioned backwards. Across from Buddy was a beautiful woman. She might have had a nice smile, but no one would have known it from the pained look on her face. Buddy kept kicking her in the knees, until he and Mom changed seats. If you ever happen to see a movie with the famous actress, Eva Marie Saint, take a close look at her knees. If they appear a little knobby, she can thank Buddy for that. Mom later said she had a very enjoyable conversation with Ms. Saint, who was flying to Japan on movie business.

As we approached Tokyo, I looked out the window to my left and saw a huge snow-capped mountain in the distance. Mom said it was the famous Mount Fuji, an active volcano. Other than the airport and the motel room, that was my only memory of mainland Japan.

The next morning, we boarded the plane for our flight to Okinawa. Two hours later, we were skirting the coastlines of the Ryukyu Islands. Below sunny skies, I glimpsed the deep dark blue of the East China Sea surrounding these islands, the largest of which was Okinawa, our new home.

The weather was similar to that of Florida, mild and slightly humid. I liked it already. One of Dad's friends picked us up at the Kadena Air Force Base airport and took us to our guest quarters. After giving us time to unpack and relax, he took us to his home and introduced us to his family. Later that afternoon he took us on a tour of the base.

Kadena Air Force Base was a beautiful, well-organized community. Part of the base consisted of runways, flight lines, hangars, offices, and maintenance buildings. This was where Dad and other military personnel worked and was mostly off limits to dependents. The rest of the base functioned as a small town, where all dependents' needs were met: housing, schools, hospital, recreational areas, commissary, retail stores, and clubs for the officers and the enlisted ranks. There was a very reliable bus system, but everything on base was within walking distance. The only problem for us was we couldn't live there—yet. Because of limited available housing, new arrivals were put on a waiting list and had to live off-base for about a year.

When Dad showed us the neighborhood we would be living in, I was dismayed. Okinawan laborers were slapping together a new batch of cracker box structures to match the recently completed houses that dotted the neighborhood. They were small, rectangular and made of cinder blocks with flimsy-looking roofs. Each house had its own septic tank in the yard, and the windows came with shutters for protection from the typhoons. The only heat came from a kerosene heater in the living room.

The Okinawans must have known what they were doing, because those houses withstood the 200-plus mile per hour typhoons we encountered that fall.

After we moved our belongings into our house, I had my first real experience with the dark side of the military class system: its privilege, arrogance, and unfairness. A knock came on our door. Standing before me was a tall, stern-looking soldier with a major's oak leaf cluster on his collar. He was wearing a beret, which indicated to me that he was a member of some type of Special Forces—obviously someone you don't trifle with.

He asked to speak to Dad. I overhead him telling Dad that this was the house he had already chosen for his family and that we would have to pack up and move to the house next door. I was a little confused since the two houses looked identical to me, but apparently this was some sort of power play. Being outranked, Dad complied with his demand without complaint, and we immediately began packing.

Our neighborhood was on a high promontory overlooking the East China Sea several miles from the base's main gate. Our house was six feet from a cliff that dropped steeply to a coral beach fifty feet below. The house wasn't much to look at, but the view was spectacular, in particular the surrounding islands in the distance, thrusting upwards out of the beautiful blue sea like tombstones in a watery graveyard. An apropos image considering the thousands of World War II dead interred in those waters. The heck with living on base—this was where I wanted to be.

The craggy coral beach, with its many tide pools, stretched almost perfectly level for several hundred yards to a sheer drop-off that led to an abyss several hundred feet deep. At low tide, the beach resembled a plateau several feet above the waterline. I loved to walk out to the end of this shelf and peer down into the briny depths, knowing I would always be treated to a wide variety of sea life. I felt like I was looking down into the deep end of a gigantic swimming pool. Beautiful, yet terrifying.

The first time I ventured out to the drop-off, I made the mistake of lingering there a little too long. While gazing into the water, I failed to notice the tide had changed and the level of the water was rapidly rising. I started casually walking back to the cliff below my house when, suddenly, the water was lapping around my ankles. I walked a little faster.

Soon, the water was up to my knees, and I was still several hundred feet from dry land. Dad had warned me to be careful, since the ebb and flow of the tides was quick and powerful.

By the time I waded ashore, the water was waist deep and still rising. After I climbed the cliff to my house and sat on the cinder block fence looking seaward, I was amazed at the transformation. Within a few short hours, the entire beach had disappeared and the waves were crashing against the base of the cliff. The water must have been at least ten feet deep where I had been standing. I learned to keep a wary and respectful eye seaward for the signs of these predictable, but fast-moving tidal changes.

I spent many enjoyable hours studying the incredible array of marine life captured in the numerous tide pools left behind at low tide. The coral was pockmarked with what looked like small craters that trapped seawater and small sea creatures until the ocean returned to release them from their temporary prisons.

While exploring the area around our house, I found a mammoth cave a quarter-mile down the beach and the mouth of a wide river a half-mile beyond that. The river was nestled between steep hills covered with dense jungle and fragrant banana trees. In those hills I discovered man-made tunnels containing spent bullets, empty brass casings, and human skulls perforated with bullet holes. Dad said we were living on the battlefield of the largest Pacific campaign of World War II—The Battle of Okinawa, which had taken place only sixteen years earlier.

During the summer, Jan, Buddy, and I spent many hours snorkeling in the crystal clear water of a shallow inlet about halfway between the cave and the river I mentioned earlier. We chased and collected sea cucumbers, sea urchins, and sea snakes. About one hundred yards from shore were several small, sheer-walled rocky islands. They were unexplorable unless one was willing to test their rock-climbing and rappelling skills.

Between tidal changes, the water between these islands was calm, but the islands' closeness to the shoreline was such that during peak changes, there was a very fast and dangerous riptide that could drag unwary swimmers out to sea. Being a brave fool, one day I decided to impress my friends with my swimming prowess by attempting to swim to one of the islands when the current was at its swiftest.

Big mistake.

The water was only about three feet deep when I started out, but halfway to the island, I realized the current was dragging me out to sea. In my panic, I took a deep breath and latched on to some outcroppings on the bottom. I managed to drag myself to shallow water and out of danger but not before ripping my fingertips to shreds on the razor-sharp coral. Shortly after that, I decided it would be a good idea to wear tennis shoes and gloves in the water; however, not before I stepped on a sea urchin, leaving my left heel looking like it had lost a duel with a porcupine.

Occasionally, we spotted the silhouettes of rusty, but still very deadly, mortars in the shallow pools at low tide, periodically washed ashore by storms. These were remnants from the several thousand U.S. and Japanese ships that were sunk offshore during the war. While we were living there, one of my schoolmates was killed when he picked up one of those live mortars. We were under strict orders to back off and notify the Base Bomb Squad whenever we discovered one.

Our neighborhood bordered a small Okinawan town, referred to as Mizu Town by the Americans, *mizu* being the Japanese word for water. This was my first experience living in a third world environment.

Next to our house was a cluster of concrete tombs containing ashes and skeletal remains of dead Japanese. Each tomb was owned and maintained by one family and was the size of a small bedroom. The entrances weren't sealed, and I occasionally snuck in and looked around. Urns containing the ashes lined the shelves alongside skulls and other bones. I'm sure the Okinawans would have been appalled at the desecration of their tombs by my presence.

On cold mornings, my chore was to take a gas can down a sloping dirt road to a small Okinawan store to buy a gallon of kerosene for our heater. Once back, I would fill the heater and light it. When the house had warmed, everyone else got up.

I loved going to that store because of the exotic candies, cookies, and other curious treats they had on display—unlike the typical things you would see in an American store. Sometimes the friendly store owner gave me free samples.

Most Okinawans lived a very rural and spartan life. I wandered through the dusty streets on the outskirts of Mizu Town, dodging the myriad bicycles and motor scooters that the locals used for transportation. Most of the few cars I saw were driven by Americans or by Okinawan taxi drivers.

A few blocks from my house was a brick factory. It was nothing more than a long, rustic wooden building containing several kilns. I sometimes sneaked in and watched Okinawan men forming the bricks in preparation for cooking in the ovens. They wore ragged shirts, shorts, and cheap rubber sandals. They went about their work with precision and good-natured chatter, with bent cigarettes dangling from their lips. From their happy expressions one would think they were at a family gathering, rather than laboring away at a dirty, sweaty job.

I was shocked to see women of all ages naked to the waist, washing their hair in the streams running alongside their shacks (most had no running water) and people relieving themselves in the wooden outhouses that straddled *benjo* (the Japanese word for toilet) ditches running with raw sewage. Pigsties built next to homes were a common sight. It was how I imagined life must have been in the United States a century earlier. Their homes looked like they would collapse at the slightest touch. These were the first to get leveled by the typhoons, but the Okinawans were resilient and rebuilt quickly.

One of the most curious sights I encountered was the strange tattoos I noticed on the backs of the hands of many of the elderly Okinawan women. There were images of flowers or animals and other indecipherable markings. At that time, I thought only sailors got tattoos. When I asked Dad about it, he told me that until the turn of the nineteenth century, it was common for young Okinawan women to get these tattoos. Some were fertility symbols while others represented family ties—a sort of archaic branding.

Occasionally, Mom and Dad took us sightseeing. One of the most memorable trips was to the Suicide Cliff Memorial in southern Okinawa. When Japan realized they were losing World War II, thousands of Okinawan civilians and Japanese soldiers jumped to their death from this cliff. They had been told by their leaders that Americans were bloodthirsty barbarians who would torture, rape, and kill their captives. This was not true but was believed because many Japanese soldiers were known to commit these same atrocities.

Soon after moving into our house, we started getting Okinawan visitors. Women and young girls, to be more precise. They didn't say much—they just spoke among themselves in Japanese—and they only showed up when Buddy and I were playing in the yard. They were friendly to Mom and Jan but were captivated by Buddy and me because of our white hair and wanted to touch it and examine it up close. Apparently, it was a novelty to them, since the only Japanese with white hair were old people. Mom and Jan had dark hair and were pretty much ignored, but they thought it was funny that the Japanese were fawning over us.

One weekend, my best friend, Don, and I went into Mizu Town and decided to shoplift from several of the crowded shops and sidewalk stalls. This phase lasted only that one summer, but it's still something that I'm ashamed of. It didn't matter what we took—we just did it for the thrill. We pocketed anything we could get our hands on: cigarettes, cigarette lighters, playing cards, cheap toys, candy.

With the confidence that came with getting away with stealing, Don decided we were going to try to steal money from one shop. I was against it, but he coerced me into joining him. The plan was for us to wait for the elderly lady behind the counter to take a break. She was working alone and, amazingly, left to visit the shop next door. Don told me to guard the front door and warn him when she returned. He slipped behind the counter, found some money in a cigar box, and grabbed it. While he was stuffing the money into his pocket, the lady abruptly returned to the shop and walked right past me.

Daydreaming, I just smiled and said "Hi." After doing a double-take, I waved at Don to warn him. Before she saw him, Don jumped out from behind the counter, grabbed me and pulled me out the door. He was so mad at me for not paying attention, I thought he was going to clobber me. We only got four dollars, but I'm sure that was a fortune to her. With the money, we bought a cheap spear gun but felt so guilty we threw it away after using it a couple of times.

I recall another reprehensible and senseless thing we did. Whenever we met an elderly Okinawan we didn't like and wanted to antagonize, we yelled, "BOOM! BOOM!" in reference to the bombings of Nagasaki and Hiroshima. From the painful and sometimes overtly hostile expressions on their weathered faces, it was obvious they knew exactly what we meant.

There was a theater in Mizu Town, a rickety wood structure that showed American as well as Japanese movies. The American movies were dubbed in Japanese. The cost of a ticket was seventeen cents. We couldn't afford that, so one day, Don and I decided to sneak in. We figured if we entered the theater an hour before show time, when no one was around, we could hide in the restroom. When the movie started, we would casually walk in undetected.

The men's and women's restrooms were two outhouses attached to the theater. There were no toilets or sinks—the theater had no running water or sewer line, just a hole in the floor over which one squatted, and a roll of toilet paper on a nail stuck in the wall.

After about twenty minutes of trying not to gag on the stench, we heard approaching footsteps. *So much for our plan,* I thought. Fortunately, it was a woman entering the outhouse next door. Luckily, no one entered the one we were in. Finally, the movie started and we snuck in and took our seats. A heck of a way to save seventeen cents, but the thrill was worth it.

Our mischievous ways caught up to us one day. While pedaling his bike with me on the back through downtown Mizu Town, Don cruised by a case of soft drinks left on the curb in front of a shop. I reached out and snatched a bottle and told Don to turn right at the corner and help me find a bottle opener. I borrowed one from a shop owner, but before I could savor that first gulp, a meaty hand clamped down on my arm. I turned, and glaring at me was the lady who owned the store from which I'd stolen the soft drink.

She jabbered away in Japanese and attracted a big crowd. She and several others grabbed me and literally dragged me back to her store. If that wasn't bad enough, she stopped every car that drove by and, jabbing her finger in my face, apparently told them what a rotten thieving American I was—which, at that moment, I was. She found someone who spoke English who explained to me that I owed her ten cents.

Don, who stood by looking as terrified as me, and I didn't have a cent between us. Her translator told me I wasn't going to be released until she got her money. I offered her what was left of the bottle, but that only made her madder.

Don offered to go home to get the money and took off. *I'll never see him again,* I thought. *And my family will probably never see me again, either.* The ensuing minutes seemed like hours. The lady continued to flag down every pedestrian, cyclist, and motorist that came by and tell her sad story. I'm surprised she didn't call the police.

By the time Don returned with the ransom, there must have been fifty people and a dozen cars tying up the intersection watching the festivities. I was beginning to feel like a prisoner of war, wondering if and when I was going to be released, but Don came through for me. After I was let go, I was afraid to venture into Mizu Town again. I also decided to retire from my life of crime.

I discovered that Okinawan boys were as crazy about baseball as I was. A group of them assembled in the afternoon to play baseball in a big field near our house. I was watching them one day from my yard, wondering aloud if they would allow an American kid to play with them.

Dad handed me my catcher's mitt and mask. "Why don't you go out there and stand off to the side and watch? Maybe they'll invite you to play."

I wandered over as Dad suggested. After a few minutes, they noticed me (they were probably more intrigued by my equipment, since most of them didn't even have gloves) and motioned me over. They made me their catcher, and I spent the rest of the day having the time of my life.

We didn't speak each other's languages, but the universal language of baseball came across loud and clear. I made some new friends that day. It was hard to believe sixteen years earlier, on this same field, those in the previous generation were killing each other in one of the bloodiest battles of World War II.

Buddy found his two new loves about this time. Across the road from our house was a rock crusher. This huge building was set into the side of a hill and produced tons of crushed rock every day. Buddy and I watched the drivers bring in truckloads of boulders and deposit them into the hopper built into the roof of the building. Inside were massive gears whose teeth would crush the boulders into gravel used for road construction.

I found it interesting, but Buddy was infatuated with the process. He would have lived inside that place had our parents let him.

His other love was the garbage collection business. He shadowed and pestered the Okinawan garbage man, who hauled off our bags of trash on his beat-up bicycle, until Mom finally put a stop to it. For some reason the man always enjoyed Buddy's company. After all, how many garbage collectors have fans?

Shoplifting wasn't the only mischief I got into with my devious, yet loyal, friend, Don. He talked me into joining him in "borrowing" a farmer's boat and rowing across the river. We discovered a field of sweet potatoes and started a fire and roasted a few over the coals. They were the best sweet potatoes I ever ate. I guess it's true that stolen fruit tastes the sweetest. It never occurred to us that what we were doing was criminal, and we were taking the food out of the mouths of this poor farmer's family.

Not only was Don a budding thief (as was I), he was the meanest and toughest boy in school. Why he liked hanging around with me was a mystery, since I was a shy, scrawny kid—maybe he just needed a sidekick, and I fit the bill. I must admit, I felt a measure of invincibility being his buddy—that is, until the toughest girl in school cleaned his clock one day at the bus stop. As usual, Don was picking on one of the smaller kids when Roxanne intervened. Don was big and built like a college football linebacker, but she was built like an NFL linebacker.

Don said the wrong thing, and the next thing I knew, he was flat on his back with Roxanne staring down at him, daring him to get up. He wisely stayed put. Don lost his bad boy reputation that day and, embarrassed to be seen with such a loser, I found myself another best friend.

One of the perks Mom enjoyed was being able to hire a live-in Okinawan maid for fifteen dollars a month. The maid cleaned and cooked. Mom even gave her free rein to tan Buddy's hide when it was warranted (which was pretty regularly). The maid was an excellent seamstress, as well. She could look at a magazine photo of a dress Mom admired and reproduce an identical one within a week.

Dad surprised us one day with his new toy: an old James motorcycle. It was made in England and looked like a piece of junk, but it ran. Dad was so proud of it, he got a helmet with his nickname on the front: WILL. Dad and I had fun cruising up and down the highway. We never knew how fast that thing could go, because the speed limit on the island was thirty miles an hour. Still, Dad managed to get a ticket. To make up for a lack of speed, Dad decided to give me a thrill by zigzagging all over the highway—until a military cop pulled us over. Mom made him get rid of it shortly after that.

After a year, our family was finally granted on-base housing. I was going to miss living in a house where I could look out my bedroom window to a beautiful panorama of the East China Sea, but I was excited about moving on-base. I was looking forward to being able to walk to all the great amenities base life provided.

Base housing was segregated: not by race, but by rank. Officers' housing, sometimes referred to as "officers' country," was located in a more upscale section of the base and the houses were bigger and much nicer than those of the enlisted ranks.

This was my first time experiencing the class system inherent in the military. In the civilian world, you can typically live wherever you want as long as you can afford it, so this separation by rank confused me. I noticed that even within "officers' country," families were separated by rank—generals, colonels, and lieutenant colonels getting larger homes on higher ground overlooking those of the junior officers.

This separation was based on the premise that officers aren't supposed to fraternize with enlisted personnel. I became friends with many kids, their parents' ranks ranging from Airman to General. Fortunately, this class baloney usually didn't extend to the kids; however, I do recall several times when an officer's kid would try to bully another kid around, claiming that his or her dad outranked their dad.

Our new house was bigger and more stylish than the one we lived in off base. A hilly, brush-covered, vacant lot was next to our house and was great fun to play in. It had a small cave where my friend, Clarence, and I went to copy each other's math homework before school every day.

For my sixth-grade science project, I decided to construct a model of our solar system. Kits weren't available then as they are in hobby shops today, so I had to design and build it from scratch. What to use for planets presented a real problem. I considered rubber balls, but the only ones I could find all looked about the same size.

While watching Mom prepare dinner one night, an idea came to me. As she peeled an onion, I noticed how evenly the outer layers came off. What started out as a large onion became a perfectly round smaller onion. If I had ten onions, I could use the largest as the sun and the remaining ones as planets. All I had to do was peel off enough layers of each individual onion to get the desired size.

I figured my teacher would probably frown on me using vegetables for this project, so I solved that problem with an idea that bordered on sheer genius. I bought several blocks of modeling clay and set to work. After peeling the onions, I carefully encased each one in a thin layer of different-colored clay to match the color of the planets as closely as possible. I now had the makings of a passable solar system.

I cut apart enough metal coat hangers to make nine rods of varying lengths to connect each planet to the sun. If all went well, no one would have a clue what was inside these beautiful orbs.

I took the whole setup to class Monday morning in pieces inside a cardboard box. I carefully inserted the metal rods into each planet, connected them to the sun, and placed it on the side table with all the other science projects.

As I stood back and admired my handiwork, I received several compliments from classmates as well as from my teacher. We were to leave them there until Friday, after which we would take them home.

I was sure I'd receive an A for my effort.

But alas, the best laid plans... Everything went great until Thursday. I came to class and noticed a foul odor. At first, I thought someone had forgotten to take a bath.

"What in the world is that smell?" my teacher asked. "Everybody check your book bags and lunchboxes. It smells like something rotten in here."

We all looked around the room, but no one could find the source of that stench. After a while, I glanced over at the science project table, and my eyes almost popped out of my head. Jupiter had suffered a major earthquake, and I knew in an instant where the smell was coming from. If you've ever smelled a rotten onion, you'll never forget it.

At the first opportunity, I surreptitiously tried to patch up the big crack that had formed when the clay had dried, but I think I just made things worse. Good thing the other planets hadn't cracked—the principal probably would have evacuated the whole school.

Friday couldn't come fast enough. I grabbed my ill-fated project and hightailed it home as fast as I could, dumping it in the first trash can I saw. By Monday, the mysterious odor had disappeared and was never mentioned again.

My best friend now was a short, feisty kid named Mickey, the son of one of Dad's best friends. Our dads were golfing buddies, and they passed on their love of the game to us.

For Christmas, 1962, my parents bought me my first set of golf clubs. Since I knew in advance I was getting them (Jan and I were notorious for unwrapping and rewrapping our presents weeks before Christmas) and couldn't stand the suspense, I set all the clocks three hours ahead. I woke Jan, Buddy, and my parents at 6:00 a.m. (really 3:00 a.m.), and we opened our presents. Mom and Dad began wondering why the sun was taking so long to rise.

After looking at his watch and seeing it was closer to 3:30 a.m., Dad looked at me in exasperation and said, "God damn it! Get back to bed and don't ever mess with those clocks again."

I slept with my clubs that morning. That beautiful set was my first love. It was just a beginner set, but it sure beat the sawed-off, hand-me-down clubs I had been using.

Mickey also got a set of clubs for Christmas, and we couldn't wait to try them. Though we played with our dads a few times, we preferred playing together on our homemade course. I would sometimes spend the night at Mickey's house, and we would get up at daybreak and head to the first tee: his front yard.

The neighbors must have hated us, because the neighborhood was our course, and their front, side, and back yards were our fairways and greens. None of the yards were fenced in, so we made liberal use of the whole area. For holes, we used empty coffee cans sunk into the ground. I lost count of how many houses we hit or the number of windows we broke. By the time anyone came outside to see what hit their house, we were on our merry way down the "fairway."

Mickey and I decided one day that we were going to become street detectives. We were fans of Sherlock Holmes and decided to use a fancy chemistry set he had to help us apprehend neighborhood criminals and bring them to justice. We had been reading up on fingerprint analysis and figured we were now experts in the field.

First, we needed a criminal. We walked around the neighborhood searching for suspicious-looking characters, but none were to be found. Okay then, we'll just look for evidence of a crime. The best we could come up with was a broken mayonnaise jar in the middle of the street. We sprung into action by cordoning off the area with some tape, then we ran to Mickey's house to get the chemistry set. We gingerly collected the broken pieces of mayonnaise-encrusted

glass and sprinkled powder where we thought fin-
gerprints would have been left. After applying tape
to the powdered glass, we looked carefully for the
prints.

Crud! Where were they? All we saw was powder. It
sure seemed a lot easier in books and on television.
Oh, well. We'll just interview the neighbors and
find out if they saw anything. The ones we talked to
looked at us as if we were nuts. Disgruntled, we sat
on the curb and pondered the case. Even if we caught
someone, how would we punish them?

Mickey came up with the bright idea of forcing
them to run around the block several times while we
rode behind them on bicycles, threatening to beat
them up if they stopped. Finally, we decided this
crime-fighting was for the birds, so we just grabbed
our golf clubs and hit the links again.

Mickey and I thought of a great way to make a little
extra money. Actually, this was our second attempt—
the first time was when his mom gave him a quarter
to get a haircut. I suggested that since I came from a
barbering family, I could do the job just as well as the
base barber and with the money we saved, we could
buy candy. This idea sounded great until I gouged a
big swath of hair from the back of his head. When his
mom found out, we lost the money, got yelled at, and
poor Mickey looked like a doofus for a few weeks.

Our second foray into the business world involved
opening a lemonade concession during the upcoming
Soap Box Derby. Started in 1934, this is an annual racing event in which homemade wooden or fiberglass

cars, piloted by a child, coast down an incline using only gravity to propel them.

Kadena Air Force Base was sponsoring a local preliminary competition and hoped to send a kid to the championship round in Akron, Ohio. We didn't care a hill of beans about the race—we were just looking to make some money.

We built a portable lemonade stand and talked our parents into buying us lemons, sugar, and paper cups. We grabbed all our supplies and equipment and set up for business next to the race track.

The day of the race was sunny and warm, and we did quite well. We probably could have added to our coffers if we had also sold Band-Aids to the kids who crashed and got skinned up. We blew all our proceeds that night on candy and fireworks, but it was an enlightening business experience.

Not far from our house was the base's east gate. Beyond that was another small town similar to Mizu Town—more of a village, actually. The main street was lined with small shops, bars and cafes. Mom took us shopping there on weekends to buy inexpensive clothes, school supplies, and toys.

The thing I liked best about this town was the abundance of fireworks shops. My friends and I went there and stocked up on firecrackers and small gunpowder-filled balls, about the size of peas, that would explode when flung against a hard object.

Our favorite ploy was to ride by street bars on a bicycle, my friend pedaling and me riding on the back with a slingshot and a pocketful of these exploding bombs. The entrances to these bars had long hallways, and when I shot the balls against the interior walls, the echo from the explosions sounded like gunshots. Immediately, people came running out into the street to see what was going on. They never did catch on that it was just two kids on a bicycle causing all that commotion.

The sidewalk cafes and vendors didn't offer the same fare one would see on American streets: hot dogs, popcorn, snow cones, etc. Among the treats they offered were dried fish on beds of rice, plates of shaved ice covered in layers of rainbow-colored powdered sugar, and unrecognizable lumps of what might have been dried fruit. I tried it all out of curiosity and was surprised to discover it wasn't bad, especially the dried fish that tasted exceptionally good.

When I grew up, I heard these small towns contained businesses that offered treats of a different variety to lonely servicemen. In Okinawa, as in other places in the Far East, massage parlors were legal and commonplace, and, in addition to massages, sexual services were surreptitiously provided at very low rates. Base commanders supposedly forbade servicemen from frequenting these places, but that didn't stop the adventurous from visiting them on the sly.

Since the military establishment wanted students to learn something about Japanese culture, it arranged for special instructors from the Japanese community to visit the schools once a week. They introduced us to subjects such as language; cooking; dancing; drama; and, my favorite, origami, the art of paper folding.

A classmate and I were assigned a project that involved hosting a dinner for the class at his house. We had to prepare, cook, and serve a typical Japanese meal and explain to the class what we were doing. I enjoyed that immensely.

One of my friend's parents invited me along to see an Okinawan play in Mizu Town. I was still interested in the dramatic arts and was curious to see a foreign play. The dialogue was in Japanese, so I had trouble following the plot, but the strange costumes and fascinating music made it a very memorable and enlightening experience.

I can still remember some of the Japanese words I learned in school as well as a few of the Japanese songs Dad taught me. One in particular was about a raccoon, and Dad liked to impress his drinking buddies by making me sing it for them. There was a time when I sang in front of cute girls. Now I was relegated to singing in front of lushes.

Part of the base's perimeter was bordered by jungle with an array of strange plants, birds, and other wildlife. I enjoyed exploring the dense tropical growth of this exotic new world and the creeks and rivers that meandered through it, but was warned to beware of the local menace: the habu, a highly poisonous snake native to Okinawa.

"One bite from a habu," Dad said, "and you're a goner."

A neighbor's dog was bitten in the face, and seeing it die in agony was something that stuck with me for a long time. I had, several days before, been crawling on my hands and knees in the same boondocks where it got attacked. That could have just as easily been me writhing around in agony on the ground. We kept our eyes open after that, but snakes didn't stop my friends or Buddy and me from playing Tarzan, king of the jungle.

One episode that stands out in my mind was the time Clarence and I decided to scare the hell out of Buddy. We had convinced him that the jungle was full of werewolves, so Buddy stuck to us like glue. As we were walking through the jungle one day, Clarence and I suddenly stopped and looked over Buddy's shoulder, opened our eyes wide and screamed, "Werewolf!" as loud as we could. When Buddy turned around, we took off running, screaming like a couple of banshees. When he saw we had left him, Buddy let out a blood-curdling yell and took off after us. We zigzagged through the jungle, still hollering, until we thought Buddy had had enough and then ran for home, my poor brother hot on our heels.

When we got to my house, Clarence and I laughed so hard we could hardly breathe. I had never seen a six-year-old kid run so fast. Of course, Buddy didn't think it was funny, and neither did Mom and Dad.

On February 26, 1962, my sister Becky was born. She was beautiful and tiny and had black hair that eventually turned blond. Buddy was relieved he wasn't the baby of the family anymore; Jan was thrilled to finally have a sister.

Jan was a sophomore in high school and was transforming from a gangly kid to a beautiful young woman. She had become more outgoing and was popular with the boys. She joined the Kubasaki High School dance team, the Falconettes. During halftime at the football games, I would proudly watch my big sister strut up and down the field.

The unusual thing about the games was Okinawa only had one high school, so it fielded two teams that played only each other. I guess you could say Kubasaki High School was perpetually undefeated.

One of the things the neighborhood kids enjoyed doing Saturday afternoons was going to the matinee at the small base theater. It always started with a cartoon, usually followed by a western or science fiction serial. The theater was always filled with boisterous kids, and the show only cost a quarter.

Afterward, we would sometimes hang out at the bowling alley (where human pin setters were poised above the rear of the alleys instead of the automatic ones used today) or visit the skating rink (where god-awful, depressing organ music played, unlike the great dance music that is heard in today's rinks).

I had my first major crush on a girl in 1962. Her name was Mary, and she lived two houses away. I was in love with her but was too scared to talk to her. I asked Mom for advice and she suggested I buy her a small gift, preferably a piece of jewelry. She took me to a small Okinawan gift shop where she helped me pick out a simple, but beautiful, inexpensive necklace. I wrapped it and contemplated how I was going to present it to Mary.

After a couple of days, Mickey told me if I didn't act soon, I might lose her. I admitted I was too scared to do it.

"You want to go over to my house for ice cream?" he asked.

"Sure," I said. The only thing I liked better than girls was ice cream.

"Go knock on her door, give her the necklace, and say, 'I love you,' and you can have all the ice cream you want."

You cruel bastard, I thought. I could almost taste the ice cream, so I agreed.

I went home, got the necklace, and stood on the sidewalk in front of Mary's house, with Mickey by my side. I don't know if he was there for moral support or if he was just making sure I kept my end of the agreement.

I slowly walked up to the door, knees shaking so badly I could barely stand. I rang the doorbell, and her mom answered.

"Um… Hi. May I please speak to Mary?" I asked.

Without saying a word, she gave me a suspicious-looking glare, turned, and walked away. A minute later, Mary was standing before me, with her mom standing behind her with folded arms.

"Alone?" I meekly said to her mom.

"Hmph!" her mom snorted, turning away, but not before fixing me with another of her beady-eyed looks.

I looked at Mary, handed her the present, blurted out, "I love you!," and turned and ran as fast as my wobbly legs could carry me.

As I flew past Mickey, I yelled, "Now where's my damn ice cream?" and kept running for his house. When we got to his house, Mickey made good on his promise. Ah! Love and ice cream. What else is there?

Oh, yeah… golf. Love, ice cream, and golf. Life was great that day!

A week later, I embarrassed the hell out of myself in front of Mary. Buoyed by my amorous feelings for her, I decided to proclaim it to the world. My platform was the bus stop near our house, a large concrete structure.

I brought a handful of chalk and wrote "Bill loves Mary" on the inside and outside walls. I was so giddy and pleased with myself, I failed to notice a bus pull up behind me. As I turned, I saw the door open and was horrified to see Mary coming down the steps. She hadn't seen me yet. I dropped the chalk and took off running up the hill behind the bus stop.

There was nowhere for me to hide, and I knew any second Mary would see me running, so I did the only logical thing: I dropped to the ground and willed myself to become invisible. Maybe she wouldn't see me. I thought it might work until I peeked out from under my arm and saw her looking back and forth between me and the bus stop. She looked puzzled, but I'm sure I detected an amused smile on her lips.

I froze. She gave me a tentative wave, and I returned it with a twitch of my hand before she turned and walked away. I felt like such an idiot.

The only other time I talked to Mary was when I walked her to school on the last day before summer vacation. Thankfully, she never mentioned the bus stop incident. I never spoke to her after that. How fleeting love is.

My family and I sat in amazement in front of the television on May 5, 1961, and watched Alan Shepard ride atop a Mercury rocket to become the first American in space. On May 25, 1961, President John Kennedy addressed Congress and proposed a national goal: by the end of the 1960's, the United States would land a man on the moon and return him safely to Earth. At first, I thought he was nuts, but then I remembered Shepard's trip into space less than three weeks earlier and decided maybe President Kennedy was right.

On July 20, 1969, Neil Armstrong became the first man to land on the Moon. Two years later, Alan Shephard became the fifth man to walk on the moon, stopping long enough to hit two golf balls on the lunar surface. That day, he became my favorite astronaut. I wonder if he thought to bring along a coffee can.

During the summer of 1962, I joined a youth baseball league, playing catcher and left field for the Giants It was the only year I played organized baseball. I enjoyed the league games, but not as much as the pick-up games with my buddies in Connecticut and my new Okinawan friends on the outskirts of Mizu town. When I entered high school and realized I wasn't good enough to make the team, I lost my interest in baseball. That fall I tried my hand at soccer, playing for the Cowboys, but wasn't any better at that than I was at baseball. I still had golf, and I wasn't planning on giving up on that.

I mentioned earlier that the dramatic world hadn't seen the last of me. I was right. Our seventh grade class was putting on a production of *The King and I*. I wanted to try out for the role of the king, but since the director (our drama teacher) decided to borrow a more mature kid from the high school for that part, I decided to try out for the part of a slave. I got the part and, even though I had no lines, I got to sing some songs with the rest of the slaves.

We rehearsed so much that I memorized the king's entire dialogue. I fantasized that on opening night the king would get laryngitis or get hit by a rickshaw or something, and the director would wail, "Oh, my God! We have no king. We'll have to cancel the play."

That would be my clue to step forward and say, in my most king-like voice, "Don't worry. I'll play the part of the king. I've memorized all of his lines."

Of course, that didn't happen, but I still had a blast singing slave songs at the top of my voice. The only problem I had with being a slave was the costume. I was naked except for my underwear and a big gold sash wrapped around my loins like an over-sized diaper. It was still better than the trapeze artist outfit from my fifth-grade play, even though I looked like a giant, yellow olive on a toothpick.

Every Sunday, Mom and Dad took us to the Officers' Club for dinner and a show, but not the kind of show you see today. The productions at the Officers' Club were extremely entertaining and were a throwback to the gala affairs you might have seen in nightclubs in the 1940's, with the exception that they were family-oriented.

Everyone dressed up in their Sunday best and sat at tables arranged in a semi-circle facing a big stage. An orchestra played popular tunes, depending on that night's theme. A master of ceremonies introduced a variety of acts. Some nights a magician would perform. Other nights there would be a comedy or singing act.

There was a spacious dance floor fronting the stage, and the guests would be encouraged to trip the light fantastic. I enjoyed watching Mom and Dad glide across the dance floor with the other parents. I'll say one thing for the military—they spared no expense in rewarding service members and their families for their hard work and sacrifice.

My favorite time came when it was the kids' turn to hit the floor for the "bell dance." It wasn't the dancing that got me fired up—it was the ritual the master of ceremonies performed during the song. At random times during the song, he would strike a bell with a small hammer, bringing the music to an abrupt halt. Immediately, waiters would carry out dishes of ice cream and hand them out to all the kids on the dance floor. If you were too timid to get out on the dance floor, you didn't get ice cream. I was a regular Fred Astaire on Sunday evenings. First, declaring my love for Mary, and now doing the jitterbug and the foxtrot in front of total strangers—it's amazing what a kid will do for ice cream.

In addition to learning more about the game of golf from Dad and his cohorts on weekends, my four-letter-word vocabulary was reaching new heights. After a round of caddying, I couldn't wait to hit the neighborhood links with Mickey so I could pass on some of those verbal gems. We idolized our dads and wanted to emulate them on the golf course.

Well, except for the gaudy, kaleidoscopic regalia they insisted on wearing. Perhaps donning this attire was their way of coping with (or rebelling against) having to wear their drab khaki uniforms the rest of the week.

I wasn't the best caddy in the world, but I worked cheap—the usual dollar a day plus all the cokes and hot dogs I could eat was still the standard. I had a hard time keeping my mouth shut when Dad was hitting his ball. One time in particular stands out. He was lined up, doing his usual pre-shot waggle and drawing his club back, when I shouted, "Hey Dad, look at that airplane!" He immediately chunked his club into the ground a good foot behind the ball, totally missing the shot. While his friends were laughing at his gaffe, he was cussing me out and chasing me across the fairway with his three wood. I picked up some choice new words on that hole to add to my repertoire.

Dad didn't hold a grudge long. On the next hole, he and I were giggling while making fun of the pre-shot waggling of one of his playing partners. I cherished those outings with Dad. I was old enough to realize that, at any time, without warning, Uncle Sam could snatch him from me and make him disappear for months at a time on one of his secret spy missions.

Seven

A Dinner Tale

When Dad was eighteen, he enjoying staying out late with his buddies. They roamed the neighborhood looking for booze, girls, or fights. Sometimes they found all three at the same time.

One night, they weren't having much luck with girls or fights, but the booze was flowing freely. They found themselves drunk on a street corner, entertaining the pedestrians with their harmonizing.

Not everyone was impressed, however, because someone called the police and complained. Before long, a night beat cop showed up and arrested them for disturbing the peace. They spent the night in jail.

Of all the irreverent and roguish deeds Dad committed in his life, the only thing he ever went to jail for was his singing. What's so ironic about that is Dad had a great singing voice—reminiscent of the late Bing Crosby.

In February, 1963, Dad received orders to report to Richards-Gebaur Air Force Base in Belton, Missouri, a small town twenty miles south of Kansas City.

I would miss Okinawa but was looking forward to new adventures, especially the opportunity to see snow again. We pulled up stakes and flew back to the States.

As before, we would have to live off-base while awaiting on-base housing. Dad found a nice two-story house in the middle of town. It had an attached one-car garage that impressed me. I had never lived in a house that had one of those. The "mansion" we rented in Connecticut had a carport, but this time our car actually had its own room. Today, most families own two or more cars and take two-car garages for granted. Back then, it was unusual for families to own more than one car, and any type of attached garage was a luxury. It didn't take me long to convert it into my personal hideaway, clubhouse, or basketball court with matching laundry hampers for baskets.

Until Dad got home from work, that is.

Jan, Buddy, and I had to provide our own entertainment for several months, because, while we flew back to the States, our furniture (including our television) was being transported by boat. We arrived with our suitcases but had to rent or buy the rest of our household items.

This was when I developed an intimate relationship with books. At night, with no television to keep me entertained, I read library books by the armload. After finishing Louisa May Alcott's *Little Women*, I decided to become a writer. I grabbed my pencil and wrote exactly two pages of the next great American novel, before I was interrupted by my friends calling me to come outside to play.

It took me only forty-eight years to resume my writing career—with the book you're now reading (although calling it the great American novel might be a bit of a stretch).

Without television's influence, I found out I actually had more fun. Our family spent more time communicating with each other, and I spent a lot more time outdoors when I wasn't devouring every book I could get my hands on. I especially loved exploring Belton with its homey, small-town atmosphere and antiquated buildings.

My biggest link to modern technology during this time was a revolutionary new device Dad bought me. Developed in 1954 and mass-produced in the 1960's, this was the newest electronic marvel: the transistor radio. It wasn't much larger than a pack of cigarettes and received AM radio signals. It came with an earphone jack and a plug-in earphone. I spent many happy hours roaming the neighborhood or lying in bed listening to the latest songs with this new-fangled gadget attached to my head.

I discovered a small lake about a half mile behind our house. It was called Lacy Lake and would soon make me a local legend (at least among my peers).

While standing on the shore one day, skipping stones across the water's surface, my friends and I wondered if anyone had ever crossed the lake on a raft. We had read Mark Twain in school and were familiar with Tom Sawyer's and Huckleberry Finn's exploits rafting down the Mississippi River. We decided to emulate our heroes by building a raft ourselves.

We collected every stick, log, board, and piece of rope we could find that wasn't already nailed down and began the task of building the raft to end all rafts. When we finished, it didn't look much like the one on which Tom and Huck navigated down Old Man River. It looked more like flotsam from a shipwreck that had collected on the shoreline.

Since none of us had any raft-building experience, nobody wanted to be the first to test its seaworthiness. Being an ex-horseback-riding daredevil who once swam fearlessly among live World War II-era mortars, I reluctantly volunteered to take the challenge.

With beaming faces and encouraging smiles, my friends pushed me to the edge of the raft and wished me luck. They also handed me a ten-foot pole to propel my way across the lake. *What if it's more than ten feet deep?* I thought to myself. Nobody knew where the bottom was.

After giving me a brisk salute (or farewell gesture), the other boys cast me off, and I was underway. After a few seconds, I realized our craft wasn't as steady as previously thought. It was about six feet square and immediately started rocking erratically. No matter how I spaced my feet, I couldn't control its motion.

To make matters worse, halfway across it started sinking. By this time, my well-wishers were running around the side of the lake yelling words of encouragement and cheering me on. I wondered if Charles Lindbergh or Alan Shepard had been as scared as I was. I somehow managed to hang on to the pole (luckily, the water was shallow enough for me to push myself forward).

After an eternity (and a tremendous balancing act), I approached the shallows of the opposite shore. By the time the raft ran aground, my friends were celebrating and shouting my name. After I jumped ashore, they nearly knocked me back into the water with their handshaking and back-slapping. From that day on, I was known as "The Legend of Lacy Lake," the boy who bravely challenged the treacherous waters of the largest lake in town.

Looking back on this, I have to laugh. What was an enormous body of water to the overactive imagination of a thirteen-year-old boy was probably no more than a large pond to an adult, and the crashing waves I encountered were most likely the ripples caused by terrified frogs scrambling to get out of my way. Even if the raft sank, I doubtless could have waded to shore. It was still a grand adventure I will always cherish.

On Sunday mornings, Dad sent me downtown to the drugstore on Main Street to buy the newspaper and a bag of horehound drops, a nasty-tasting candy that, apparently, only old people cared for. Like Wallingford and Winter Haven, Belton was a small town where everything was within walking distance. Before returning home from my errand, I usually visited the various stores and wandered among the railroad tracks that bisected the town. Good thing he didn't send me for ice cream.

After a year, we were granted on-base housing. Once again, I was able to enjoy all the great amenities provided on base. We moved into a small duplex with a carport on a street with other junior officers. As on Kadena Air Force Base, family housing here was segregated by rank: the higher the rank, the nicer the house.

Cutting across the residential area was a major road separating the officers' houses from those of the enlisted ranks. The enlisted families lived in quadplexes similar to the one we occupied in The Cabbage Patch. Of course, the senior officers had their large, single-family houses befitting their status. I was still too young to understand the reasoning behind this, but the memory of this same class discrimination I witnessed in Okinawa had left a negative impression on me.

My new friend, Greg, convinced me to join his Boy Scout troop. At fourteen, I was a little self-conscious about being the oldest Tenderfoot in the troop, so I worked on earning my Second-Class badge as soon as I could. We went on a quite a few campouts and hikes (several were twenty miles) along country roads, forest trails, and up some pretty steep mountains. They were enjoyable, but camping in freezing weather was a real challenge. It was nice seeing snow again, even though I was trudging through it instead of sledding on it.

When we weren't camping with our troop, Greg and I honed our camping skills by pitching a tent in his backyard on weekends. The most important lesson we learned was not to pitch a tent directly beneath the eaves of a house during a torrential rainstorm. We made that mistake one night, and our tent came crashing down on top of us, leaving us and all our gear soaking wet. We went back into his house looking like a couple of drowned rats.

Greg and I continued our Tom and Huckleberry phase by lounging around our tent smoking home-made corncob pipes. Well, they weren't actually made from corncobs. We made them from sawed-off, hollowed-out sections of a broomstick with drilled-out pieces of dowel rod glued to their sides. They made fairly decent, functioning pipes. Our carpenter skills weren't that great, so they had a tendency to fall apart easily. We snuck cigarettes from our parents, tore them apart and packed our pipes full of tobacco. They made us nauseous, but it was still fun. Too bad they didn't give out merit badges for pipe-making.

The scouting hikes and campouts were fun, but I quit after two months. I got tired of the occasional teasing of classmates when I wore my uniform to school as well as taking orders from eleven-year-old kids who still outranked me. At least the scoutmaster didn't segregate our tents and sleeping bags by rank on our campouts.

I nearly got Dad in serious hot water with the base commander. Greg and I were walking home from the movies one day and decided to take a detour through an enlisted men's barracks. We weren't looking for trouble, we just wanted to see what their quarters looked like.

We were strolling down an empty hallway when one of the residents came out of his room and yelled,

"What are you kids doing here? This place is off limits."

I panicked and froze, but Greg started running. The man grabbed me, and to his credit, Greg came back. He could have escaped but instead, he chose to stand by his friend and face the music.

Since we were teenagers, the man was sure we were juvenile delinquents and accused us of looking for something to steal. We tried to convince him we were just trespassers, not thieves. He didn't believe us and called the military police. I guess the police believed our story, because they let us go after taking our names, addresses, and phone numbers down to the station. They said they weren't going to take us in, but, instead, were going to notify our parents.

If they had suspected us of stealing, they might have arrested us, which would have had serious repercussions on Dad's career. Base commanders didn't tolerate questionable behavior from their subordinates or their dependents. Neither did Dad—I got a pretty good whipping that night.

One beautiful Sunday morning, Dad shelved his Sunday golf game and announced we were all going for an afternoon drive in our brand-new, 1964 Ford Galaxy 500. With baleful groans, Jan, Buddy, and I filed into the backseat of the car with Becky sandwiched between us.

"Make sure you wear clean underwear," Mom said. "Just in case we get into an accident."

I could just picture the scene at the emergency room: The doctor saying, "Your kids are pretty mangled up, Mr. and Mrs. Willis."

And the nurse piping in, "Yeah, but they sure have on nice clean underwear, don't they?"

Off we went into the scenic Missouri countryside, Jan in a snit because she couldn't be with Delbert, her new boyfriend, and Buddy and I picking at each other out of boredom, all the while listening to my parents' incessant proclamations of "Oooh... look at that big red barn!"

"Wow... check out that old silo!"

"Look, kids. A cow!"

I was beginning to think an accident wouldn't be so bad if it got us out of this miserable expedition through rural purgatory. I guess Mom and Dad must have felt a little guilty, because our trips usually ended with a stop at the Dairy Queen for ice cream. Maybe these trips weren't so bad after all.

During the summer of 1963, we drove up to Minneapolis, Minnesota, to visit Dad's sister, Mary Mayes, and her family for several days. It was beautiful there, but quite a bit cooler than in Missouri.

My cousin, Rusty, worked weekends as a caddy at a posh country club and asked me if I'd like to caddy with him Saturday morning. He had cleared it with the caddy master and said I would earn three dollars plus a tip if I did a good job. Since I had a lot experience caddying for Dad, I thought it was a great idea.

We showed up and were assigned to a couple of guys who reeked of money. *This sure is a step up from the Kelly Golf Course*, I thought to myself.

The only drawback was that we couldn't use a pull cart as I had done with Dad. I had to carry that heavy bag over my shoulder like the pros did.

I had fun caddying, but was surprised that the golfers didn't use the same colorful language Dad and his partners used. My golfer bought me cokes and hot dogs, and I was making three times what Dad paid me. I was moving up.

After the round, I received my three-dollar fee plus a two-dollar tip. I thought I was rich. To top it off, they even let us swim in the club's private swimming pool. The water was ice cold, but we had a blast.

We were watching *The Jack Paar Program* one evening, and he had a segment about a new phenomenon occurring in Liverpool, England. A film crew had been sent over there to record a popular rock 'n' roll group taking the local music scene by storm. In the filmed segment, I saw four scruffy-looking guys with unkempt hair, tight jeans, cowboy boots, and leather jackets. They called themselves The Beatles.

They hadn't made their breakthrough in the United States yet, and though I had never heard of them, I thought their unique sound was pretty cool. A month later on February 9, 1964, they made their live American debut on *The Ed Sullivan Show*. I immediately became hooked on their music along with the rest of America's teenagers.

That same year, another British band, The Rolling Stones, hit it big as well. This British invasion took a lot of the steam from American rock 'n' roll bands, especially The Beach Boys, who had dominated the music scene for several years.

My cousin, Rusty, and his family visited us from Minneapolis about that time. What was memorable about that visit was what he brought with him: an acoustic guitar. The year before, he had visited and brought with him a ukelele, on which he taught me the basic chords. I wasn't too impressed with it. The guitar was a lot cooler, but we weren't too sure what to do with the two extra strings. Neither of us had much success with it at first, but it did spark an interest in music in both of us.

My new-found interest in the guitar and the advent of this new era in rock 'n' roll had a profound effect on me for the next twenty years.

Dad reinforced my love of fishing while living in Missouri by taking me along with him and his buddies to several of the local lakes and rivers. One incident stands out in my mind. We usually used rods and reels, but this time Dad also brought along a ten-foot cane pole. He tied on a line, baited the hook, and propped it up with rocks on the bank.

Not paying too much attention to the cane pole, he cast another line into the water. I glanced over just as the end of the cane pole dipped a few times and then took off like a rocket. I don't know what took the bait, but it was fast. I yelled, and Dad and I watched that pole shoot across the lake like a torpedo, then suddenly stop, jerk upright for a few seconds, and disappear straight down into the depths.

Dad and I looked at each other and nearly fell in the water, we were laughing so hard. That must have been some fish, because we never saw that pole again.

Another new friend, Bobby, and I decided to get up early one Saturday morning to go fishing at a lake on the north side of the base. This lake contained a small, round, tree-covered island about fifty feet in diameter. We knew the lake was shallow, so when we arrived at the shore at daybreak, we stripped down to our underwear and, holding our clothes and fishing gear above our heads, waded through the chest-deep water to the island.

We caught several perch, the largest no more than several inches long. We didn't care how big they were. After scaling and cleaning them, we fried them in my Boy Scout collapsible frying pan over a small fire. It wasn't a big meal, but those fish were delicious, almost as good as the bluegill Dad and I caught in Wallingford. Afterward, Bobby and I relaxed with a couple of puffs on my corncob (I mean broomstick) pipe.

I was becoming more and more interested in girls around this time but was still awkward and painfully shy around them. Bobby announced he was going to throw a party at his house in a few weeks. I was excited about going until he told me there was going to be dancing... with girls. Gulp!

To me, a party was a fun event where you ate cake, drank punch, ogled girls, and hung out with the guys.

Bobby explained this was a teen party with music, and the girls would expect to be asked to dance.

I didn't like the sound of that, but he said dancing was mandatory. After I told him I didn't know how to dance, he said he would teach me enough to get by. Not wanting to miss out on the party, I spent the afternoon in his basement trying not to stomp on his toes while he taught me the latest dance moves.

The jitterbug was still in fashion, but a popular dance, the twist, was all the rage. He showed me some basic steps, and I figured I could fake the rest. I'm sure glad his parents didn't come home and catch the two of us dancing around together. That could have damaged our rough-and-tumble (in our minds, at least) reputations.

The night of the party, I was extremely nervous. Bobby practically had to threaten to beat me up before I finally asked a girl to dance. I couldn't get the hang of the jitterbug, but I quickly caught on to the twist. *This ain't so bad*, I thought. When a slow song came on, panic set in. I had never slow-danced before and wasn't even sure how to hold my partner. Apparently, she knew what she was doing and wrapped her arms around me. After a few awkward moments, I started enjoying it. It was a lot easier, too. My apprehension was gone and replaced by a new sensation. It looked like this was going to be a pretty good party after all.

All we did that night was dance, but that was a big turning point in my life. I bid farewell to Tom and Huck, because it now appeared that greater adventures were around the bend for this boy—or young man, I should say.

After that night, I looked forward to these parties and soon became a pretty good dancer, mastering the jerk, the frug, the swim, the mashed potato, and the pony (the latest dance moves). I even won a twist contest at another party a few months later.

A popular pastime among kids was roller skating. The only skates available, outside of skating rinks, were the weighty, metal kind with brackets on the sides. The brackets were used to clamp the skates onto leather shoes with a skate key. They were very cumbersome, and if the nuts and bolts weren't kept tightened, the skates were notorious for coming apart just when one hit top speed on a bumpy street or sidewalk. The vibration from the metal was enough to rattle one's teeth.

Dad told me how, when he was a kid, he and his friends took skates apart and nailed the front and back halves to the bottoms of wooden orange crates. These crates made nice carts for racing down hilly streets. They usually broke apart after a few runs, but during the Great Depression, kids had to make do with what they had.

His stories inspired my friends and me to take it a step further. We took the skates apart and threw the shoe platforms away. What remained were the brackets holding the front and rear wheels which we screwed to the front and rear ends of a foot-long two-by-four. Even though California surfers had, since the 1950's, been experimenting with attaching skates to wooden boxes and boards, we may have built the prototype of the modern skateboard.

There was barely enough room on the board for our feet, but we found out by keeping the board short, we could do hairpin turns at full speed down a steep slope. We were leaping over curbs and crashing and burning years before Tony Hawk was even born.

I decided to impress a girl I liked with my skateboarding skills. When the school bus approached my house one morning, I saw her sitting in her usual seat by a front window. Before it pulled up, my plan was to zoom down my driveway, execute a flying leap over the curb, and follow that with a successful landing in front of the bus.

Really stupid idea.

Everything was going great, until I hit the curb. My feet flew out from under me, causing me to land flat on my back. I flung the skateboard onto my porch and boarded the bus amid catcalls and laughter. I don't know what hurt worse—my pride or my back, but instead of quitting while I was behind, I kept practicing until I got my landing right.

I mentioned I was a Boy Scout for two months. During that time we had a Christmas card drive, in which we were each given a dozen boxes of Christmas cards to sell. I wasn't too keen on door-to-door sales, but I had no choice. We wouldn't be paid, but if we sold all twelve boxes, we would get to choose a prize from a select list.

Off I went with my cards and met immediate rejection. Slightly discouraged, I trudged up to the next door. Same result. *This stinks!* I thought. After an hour of rude receptions or watching people peek through their curtains at me like I had leprosy, I returned home, dejected.

Mom knew I was feeling pretty low, and she knew how much I wanted to win one of those prizes. She sat next to me and gave me one of the best pep talks about perseverance I had ever heard. Buoyed by her enthusiasm and confidence in me, I decided to give it another try. I sold all twelve boxes and walked in the house grinning from ear to ear. I found Mom and gave her a big hug and thanked her for not letting me quit.

When I saw the list of prizes I could choose from, I couldn't believe my eyes. One of the prizes was a genuine brass bugle. Since I already knew how to play the trumpet, I figured mastering this gleaming beauty would be a piece of cake.

When I got the bugle and showed it to Dad, he seemed impressed. Mom, on the other hand, didn't look too happy. Considering the racket I had made with my trumpet five years earlier, I could just imagine what she was thinking: *What the hell have I done?*

I could also picture her banging her head against the kitchen cabinet, as I strolled merrily through the neighborhood blaring out "Taps," "Reveille," and any other bugle calls I could think of.

During the summer, one of Dad's friends invited us up to his lakeside cabin in the Lake of the Ozarks, located in the middle of the Ozark Mountains. His friend had a boat and was going to teach us to water ski. I had never heard of a mountain having a lake, but there it was—a long, shallow pristine lake snaking through beautiful, tree-lined peaks. I had a lot of fun learning to water ski and was soon hooked. It was more fun than skateboarding and hurt a lot less when I fell.

Since my friends and I were now more interested in girls than sports, my golf clubs went into early retirement. I still caddied for Dad occasionally when I needed spending money, but it wasn't until a decade later that my interest in the game was rekindled.

As an officer as well as an excellent golfer, weekly outings with his superiors became almost a requirement for Dad. He hit the links at least twice a week, occasionally with the base commander. He became so consumed with the sport, he wrote a weekly column that appeared in the base newspaper. Titled *Once Upon a Tee*, it chronicled his golf exploits on and off base and was also a soapbox for his feelings and opinions about golf. His column included a flattering picture of himself holding a club.

Two world-changing events occurred during this time. One was the debut of the 1965 Ford Mustang in March, 1964. This breathtaking, revolutionary car took the automotive world by storm.

My friends and I marveled at its sleek design, and we all vowed to own one someday. One of my teachers actually had the audacity to say this unique, future classic was the ugliest car she had ever seen.

Lee Iacocca, the former president of Ford, wrote in his autobiography that the car was named for the P-51 Mustang fighter plane made famous in World War

II, and not the horse. I guess Ford decided the horse emblem on the chassis would be more attractive and marketable than an outdated plane.

The other event was the assassination of President John F. Kennedy on Friday, November 22, 1963, in Dallas, Texas. I remember sitting in English class when an announcement came over the PA system saying the President had been shot while riding in a motorcade in Dealey Plaza.

My teacher was so upset she started sobbing uncontrollably. Shortly after, another announcement stated that the President was dead. By now, most of the girls in class were crying as well, and all the boys had shocked looks on their faces. This was only my second experience with death, after that of Granddad's passing in 1960.

Dad took the President's assassination especially hard. He loved Kennedy and all he stood for—especially the way he stood up to the Soviet Union's Nikita Khrushchev during the Cuban Missile Crisis of 1962. I remember watching the funeral procession on television, especially the image of three-year-old John Kennedy, Jr. saluting his dad's casket.

Fourteen months later, I would be enrolling in John F. Kennedy High School in San Antonio, Texas. Built in 1963, this was the first school named after the president. Ironically, on November 21, the day before he was killed, he had visited San Antonio and promised to return to dedicate the new school named in his honor.

My next experience dealing with death hit a little closer to home. In the spring of 1964, Grandpa and Grandma Frier began a road trip to visit us in Missouri. They made it about halfway but had to turn back when Grandpa experienced chest pains. Grandma took him to the hospital, where he died shortly afterward, on May 23, from lung cancer.

We were devastated. I had been especially looking forward to seeing them again. Memories of all the great times Grandpa and I had together came flooding back, especially the long walks we took along the railroad track near his house, silently enjoying each other's company.

Just when I was learning my way around the base and had made a lot of friends, Dad got new orders. He said we were going to Brindisi, a small town on the southeast coast of Italy, overlooking the Adriatic Sea. For several weeks, I was excited about going overseas again, but that ended when his orders were changed.

Because of a reduction in force (RIF in military jargon) of reserve officers, of which Dad was one (since he never earned a college degree), he was going to be forced into retirement. As a captain with twenty-two years of service, he qualified for a full pension. The only problem was he was slated for promotion to major in December. If he retired immediately, he would never make it to major, causing him to lose out on a substantially larger pension.

Dad was not ready to give up just yet, despite the dilemma. He appealed to his superiors to be allowed to stay active for another six months. The Air Force gave him a solution that allowed him to do that, albeit a costly one (in the short term, at least). On his scheduled discharge date, he gave up his reserve officer status and reverted to technical sergeant, the enlisted rank he held before he went to Officers Candidate School.

The Air Force was RIFing out reserve officers, not technical sergeants, and this was his loophole. All he had to do was put up with a cut in status and pay for six months until his scheduled promotion date arrived, and then he would be allowed to retire as a major.

It didn't make much sense to me (and still doesn't), but when I joined the military five years later, I learned that military logic and common sense don't always go hand-in-hand.

The one bright spot in all of this was where we'd be living during Dad's last tour of duty: Marathon, Florida. This small town is located in the Florida Keys, just off the southern coast of Florida. Dad was being assigned to the Naval Air Station at Key West, where his outfit was given the responsibility of monitoring radio transmissions from communist Cuba and protecting our national security. The Cuban Missile Crisis had made the world a more perilous place, and constant vigilance from the Communists was now a top national priority.

Holy cow... another island? I couldn't get packed fast enough, but all this moving was beginning to get to Mom. To make matters worse, she was mortified and livid when the base inspection team came to our house, just before we left, and gave it a white-glove inspection. Saying we failed the inspection, they demanded we clean the house all over again. If Dad had not interfered, I'm sure Mom would have sent a couple of those inspectors to the hospital. By now, she was getting fed up with military life and was looking forward to settling down after Dad's retirement in December. After being the dutiful, supportive military wife for nineteen years, she deserved that.

Eight

❦

A Dinner Tale

Dad's love of fishing began as a kid living in Portsmouth, Virginia near the Atlantic coast. He may have inherited this trait from Granddad, who once worked as a fisherman. Not the romantic seafaring kind you read about in Ernest Hemingway novels, but the kind who did whatever it took to put food on the table.

Granddad was part of a crew whose job was to climb out on tree branches that overhung a river, while carrying cast nets on their backs. Another crew, making as much noise as they could, "herded" schools of fish under the tree, and Granddad and his partners leaped into the water and captured as many fish as they could in the nets.

Dad took a more traditional approach to fishing. One day, he and a pal rented a small motorboat and headed out to sea. Things were going well until the motor died. Dad checked the sparkplug. Cardinal rule when checking the sparkplug: Don't drop the sparkplug overboard!

Dad dropped the sparkplug overboard.

They had no paddle, and the boat started drifting out to sea. Eventually, a Coast Guard boat came by, threw them a line, and towed them to shore.

Maybe he would have been better off if he had tried fishing from a tree like Granddad.

Blue water. On both sides of the highway, as far as the eye could see. In the distance, sailboats were tacking with their colorful mainsails in stark contrast to the shimmering light reflected from the whitecaps. The turquoise water near the shore was surprisingly clear and changed to ever-darkening shades of blue as the shallow water gave way to the increasing depths of the Florida Straits. The sun's rays glinted off the surface and stung my eyes, and the salty air crusted our windows and teased my senses.

Dad explained that the Florida Keys were a long series of subtropical islands, made up mostly of sand and coral and festooned by lush mangrove trees as well as towering coconut palms. Many of the keys connected to others by bridges, but most just decorated the Florida Straits like isolated jewels on a blue velvet surface, uninhabited and covered in dense foliage. Highway 1 bisected the Florida Keys and ended in Key West.

The picturesque town of Marathon had a population of around two thousand and stretched across a dozen or so irregularly-shaped keys. It was located one hundred miles south of Miami and thirty-five miles from Key West. The house my parents rented was on Vaca Key.

Several hundred yards past the bridge bringing us onto Vaca Key, we turned right onto a gravel road leading to our new home. The house was small, but the back yard fronted a canal leading into the open sea. We were closer to the water than we were when we lived near Mizu Town, Okinawa. Our house was in a small neighborhood with a grocery store, a few bars, and a bunch of souvenir shops.

Directly across the highway was the Jack Tar Lodge, a place which soon became a regular hangout for Buddy and me. It had an enormous pool that we were allowed to use for fifty cents per day, plus a great game room.

The biggest draw, however, was the Lodge's marina, where a vast assortment of boats were docked. Buddy and I loved to wander the docks, looking at the enormous, gleaming yachts and weather-beaten fishing boats and checking out the catches of the returning fishermen. Sometimes they would give us the fish they didn't want, and Mom would always yell at us for bringing those smelly nasty things into the house.

The largest and most impressive charter fishing boat was the *Captain Winner*, whose owner surprised me with a phone call one day. We had never met, but I had been referred to him by his neighbor, whose lawn I had just mowed the previous weekend. I couldn't have been more impressed if the President of the United States had made that call. He wanted me to mow his lawn, but instead of paying me the three dollars that I usually charged, he offered me a free ticket for an all-day fishing cruise on his boat. I jumped at the chance and had the time of my life rubbing elbows with the rich tourists. The crew could tell I had no idea what I was doing, but they treated me well and taught me the basics of deep-sea fishing. I've been hooked ever since.

Mom gave birth to John that August and didn't get out of the house much. Jan had just graduated from Belton High School that May and moved to Florida with us. She found a part-time job at the Kwik Chek grocery store around the corner of our house. She was a big help to Mom, especially since Becky was two years old and needed supervision.

It was obvious from the beginning that Jan was miserable. She had no boyfriend nor career plan, and the prospect of finding either one on this desolate island was slim.

After a few months, she moved to Winter Haven to live with Grandma. With Grandpa gone, Grandma was lonely and appreciated the company. Jan found a job as a clerk in a five-and-dime store downtown. She couldn't afford a car but didn't need one in that small town. She made friends fast and started dating again. She was enjoying the life of a young single girl, but living with Grandma was beginning to cramp her style.

When Dad wasn't working, he was drinking with co-workers at the neighborhood bars in Key West and Marathon or drag racing his Galaxy 500 on the private air strip a few blocks from our house. Dad didn't seem to be very interested in hanging out with his family in those days. I realized later that being at home with a bunch of kids was a bit overwhelming for Dad. He was a good father, but, at forty-one, he was still a little self-absorbed and carefree. Until the day he died, Dad was a kid at heart who seemed to think life was a game to be enjoyed at all costs, until the final buzzer sounded.

We were pretty much on our own the summer Buddy was eight years old and I was fourteen. I kept an eye on him when I could. No one kept an eye on me. We had our own friends, but we still spent a lot of time together. We spent most of the summer roaming the neighborhood, checking out the fishing action at the marina, and exploring the canals and the bridge connecting Marathon to the island to the north. We rarely wore anything other than t-shirts, shorts, and flip flops and were in the water every chance we got.

I'll never forget the time Buddy cost me my precious BB gun. He snuck up on the driver's side of the mailman's truck, stuck the gun in his face, and yelled, "Stick 'em up!"

The mailman grabbed it and told Buddy if he wanted it back, he would have to tell his dad to pick it up at the Sheriff's office. I never saw that gun again.

The atmosphere in Marathon was laid back and un-hurried. The friendly locals appeared to be living in a time warp—nobody seemed to be in a hurry, and most of the ones I met didn't seem too concerned with what was happening on the mainland. I believe the reason so many people migrated to the Florida Keys was to escape and to be left alone, a prime example being Ernest Hemingway, who spent the most productive years of his writing life in Key West.

The local hangout in our neighborhood was a seedy-looking bar called the Dog House. Dad spent many evenings there soaking up the local atmosphere (as well as the booze), hobnobbing with his new-found neighbors. The name was appropriate, since he was usually in the dog house when he came staggering home late at night. I always felt Dad earned the right to unwind a little after a busy day of spying on Fidel Castro's activities.

I had found that the water along the docks yielded treasures for the taking. Not gold, nor silver, nor even pearls. These treasures were the glass soft drink bottles that vacationers tossed away when they were empty. (I'm sure the locals had more respect for the island than to litter.) Those bottles were worth two cents apiece, which was a lot to a kid.

My friends and I dove into the clear shallow water and scavenged as many bottles as we could find. The chipped bottles we tossed into trash cans; the rest we cleaned and returned to a local store for cash. Cleaning the barnacle-encrusted bottles was hard work, but being broke most of the time and desperate for pocket money, we persevered.

When our treasure-hunting venture slowed, we resorted to another way to supplement our income. We noticed that, after giving us our money for the empties, the owner of the store put the bottles out back in a fenced-in yard. We waited until he re-entered the store, then quickly hopped over the fence and grabbed the same bottles we had just turned in.

We jumped the fence again and went back into the store for another refund on those same bottles. The third time we did this, he wised up and realized what was going on. He ran us off, threatening to call the cops. It was about this time I figured I would be better off if I stuck to an honest (but not nearly as much fun) means of making money: mowing lawns.

One of Dad's favorite stories he loved to tell was of the time he and a friend were cruising up Highway 1, returning to Marathon from Key West. Just before the cutoff to our house, Dad's friend started laughing.

"Look at that crazy little kid, dragging that big fish across the highway. It's bigger than he is."

Dad started laughing as well, then slowed down and yelled, "Hey, that's my kid!"

It was Buddy, bringing home a fish that one of the fishermen at the Jack Tar Lodge had given him. Dad pulled off the highway and told Buddy to get his butt home. I don't remember if Dad told Buddy to get rid of his catch of the day or if he had Mom cook it up for dinner.

Two brothers, who were friends of mine and Buddy's, lived across the canal from us and had access to their dad's boat, a sweet thirteen-foot Boston Whaler. I thought being a kid and entrusted with your dad's boat was the coolest thing. They took us out in the shallow bays and the mangrove swamps along the shore, where we would fish and gig for flounder, or when Buddy got the chance, raid other people's lobster traps.

That September, after performing in Montreal, The Beatles headed for a concert in Jacksonville, Florida. Because Hurricane Dora was wreaking havoc on the east coast, their flight was diverted to Key West for a short layover. They were at the height of their popularity, and by this time, I was a devout Beatles fan. When I heard they might pose for photos, I begged my parents to take me to Key West to see my idols. They refused, but my classmate Darlene talked her parents into taking her. Before she left, I asked her to get me the group's autographs. She promised she would get them.

The next day, I was amazed when I saw the front page of the local newspaper. There was a big picture of Darlene with one arm around Paul McCartney's neck and the other arm around John Lennon's neck. That night, after the storm passed, The Beatles flew on to Jacksonville. After that, Darlene was a school celebrity. Optimistically, I asked her where my autographs were. She said she forgot to ask for them. Yeah … I'm sure she did.

Before school started, Mom decided to send me to Hollywood, Florida, to spend a week with her sister, Teeny Moxley, and her husband, Smoky. The bus trip up there was almost as memorable as the visit.

I got lost.

At fourteen, I had never traveled anywhere by myself. Mom told me to get off at the Fort Lauderdale bus terminal, where Uncle Smoky and Aunt Teeny would be waiting for me. The bus trip took about an hour, and I got off at the first stop, not realizing that the bus made several stops along the way.

I assumed I was in Fort Lauderdale. I was wrong— I was in Coral Gables, several miles south of my destination. I waited for three hours, wondering if my relatives had forgotten about me. I got scared and finally asked another bus driver if this was Fort Lauderdale. When he told me it wasn't, I almost cried. He said he was headed to Fort Lauderdale and would take me there.

When I finally arrived, Uncle Smoky and Aunt Teeny were worried and upset. They said they were about to give up and go home. If they had, there's no telling what would have happened to me.

They had always treated me well and were fun to be around, but Uncle Smoky was a real blast to hang out with, because he was almost as wild as Dad. An ex-Navy man, he was an aircraft mechanic at the Miami airport and loved to spend his spare time tinkering with an old, souped-up Volkswagen Beetle he kept in the garage.

The Moxleys were the only people I've ever known who had an airplane in their backyard. Well, not the whole plane, just the fuselage and wings. Uncle Smoky had a pilot's license and had access to several single-engine airplanes at the airport. He told me the owners let him borrow them occasionally in exchange for working on them. I never knew if he was working on the one in the yard or if he placed it there to impress (or irritate) the neighbors.

The week I was visiting, Uncle Smoky let me ride with him while he raced his Beetle around town. The way he drove, he must have thought he was in the Grand Prix. I wonder if he ever noticed the holes I dug in the dashboard with my fingernails.

We had a great time together. He had two daughters, Janie and Vickie, and was crazy about them, but sometimes I think the extra attention he gave me was because he looked upon me as the son he never had.

Another great experience I had that week was when he took me for a ride in his friend's single-engine airplane. After zigzagging between the coastline and the countryside, he decided to give me a thrill by buzzing his house. He went into a steep dive and pulled up seconds before coming within fifty feet of his roof. I couldn't wait to tell my friends about that exciting adventure. I wonder if the owner of the plane ever noticed the holes I dug in the cockpit's control panel with my fingernails.

Uncle Smoky and Dad got along like brothers, because they had so much in common. Dad had been an aircraft mechanic before he became an officer, and their penchant for drinking, irreverence, contempt for authority, and their devil-may-care attitude gave them a special bond.

Upon hearing of Uncle Smoky's passing years later, I was terribly saddened. With his swooping, handlebar mustache, he was truly an anachronism, born one hundred years too late. The best way to describe him is to compare him to Gus, a character from Larry McMurtry's novel, *Lonesome Dove*. He lived life by his own rules and wasn't afraid to kick someone's butt if provoked.

Uncle Smoky came to visit us in San Antonio in the 1970's. He, Dad, Buddy, and I went golfing, and as we were turning into our neighborhood, someone cut us off. Buddy was driving and Uncle Smoky was sitting next to him. Words were exchanged between the other man and Uncle Smoky, who by this time was hanging out the window, waving his fists. Uncle Smoky wanted Buddy to follow the guy so he could drag him out of his car and beat him up. What a character—I still miss him.

During my visit to Fort Lauderdale, they took me to a lake resort several miles inland. They rented a cabin for a few days, and I got the chance to water ski again. After skiing, I looked down from the dock and saw a six-foot-long alligator sunning himself on the bank. I asked Uncle Smoky if there were a lot of alligators here.

"Oh yeah, they're all over," he said. "Hee-hee; good thing you didn't fall while you were skiing. Ready to go again?"

"Uh, no thanks," I replied in a queasy voice. I had forgotten what Grandpa said four years ago about Florida's lakes teeming with alligators.

I was introduced to the most amazing sight I had ever seen while at this resort. One of the neighbors invited us over to see the latest technological phenomenon. When I walked into his living room, he pointed to a television. Not just any television, but one that showed color images. I had heard rumors about this new invention but had never seen it. I don't remember what show was on, but I sat there, enthralled. It was like being at the movie theater. *Wait until my family hears about this!*

Buddy and I loved to wander the island and swim in the warm waters of the Florida Straits. The pool at the Lodge was fun but wasn't as exciting as swimming in the canals and off the docks. I spent many afternoons sitting on the edge of the canal in our backyard, trying to catch the numerous, beautiful parrotfish that swam below my feet. Mom sometimes had to yell at me several times, waking me from my sun-induced reverie, to remind me to come in for dinner. I vowed that I would someday own my own house on a canal where I could wile away the time fishing with my kids and grandkids.

My friend, Jimmy, and I got the crazy idea to jump off the bridge that connected Marathon Island to its northernmost neighbor, Fat Deer Key. This bridge was about twenty-five feet high, and he and I spent hours leaping into the clear blue water. Jumping was dangerous, since, during tidal changes, the current was extremely fast. I remember jumping when the current was at its swiftest and paddling like hell to get to the shore before being pulled out to sea. Mom would have been furious if she had known I was risking my life like that.

The current wasn't the only danger when jumping. One time, just as Jimmy leapt from the bridge, I looked down and spotted a four-foot long barracuda eye-balling us. I pointed and screamed, "Barracuda!" at the top of my lungs, and Jimmy started kicking his legs and windmilling his arms as if he were trying to fly back to the bridge. When he hit the water, he looked like Tarzan trying to outswim a hungry crocodile. I swear he broke the world record for the fifty-meter freestyle that day.

My screaming must have scared the barracuda even more, because it took off like a bolt of lightning and was probably in Cuban waters even before my friend hit the water.

I decided to pick up where I left off in Connecticut regarding my Olympic track star aspirations. Not wanting to waste time on that lame high jump stuff, I decided to think big. The 1964 Olympics was underway that fall, and the pole vault event caught my eye.

I can do that, I thought.

Jimmy and I talked his mom into picking us up a sturdy, ten-foot bamboo pole while she was on a shopping trip to Miami. I don't know how she got it in (or on) her car, but it was a real beauty. I knew Olympians had switched to fiberglass poles that year, but bamboo was all we could afford.

We built our pole vaulting apparatus much like the high jump setup I had in Connecticut, except the two-by-fours used to hold the crossbar (a dowel rod this time, not a broom handle) were eight feet long.

We pounded nails into the two-by-fours at one-inch intervals to hold the crossbar. We still weren't sure if the pole would even hold our weight, so, being the daredevil (or village idiot) that I was, I volunteered to go first.

After stomping a hole into the grass with my heel (to catch the bottom of the cane pole), I was ready for takeoff. I backed off fifty feet, held the pole the way the experts did and started sprinting for glory. At the precise moment, I planted the pole in the depression I had made in the grass. Only one problem—while pulling myself up, I noticed my body was moving forward and under the bar instead of over it. I glanced down and realized the pole had missed it's mark and was now skittering across the grass.

I let go of the pole and, with arms and legs akimbo, landed hard on my left side. Unfortunately, my left forearm was under me as I hit, and there was a loud crack! I jumped up and noticed my arm wasn't hanging right—it looked more like the letter "Z" than an arm. It didn't hurt yet—apparently, shock had set in.

Jimmy freaked out and went to get Mom. She and Jan came out, and when they saw me, they started shrieking and running around in circles. I was the calmest one there.

Mom finally gathered her wits and drove me to the Fisherman's hospital where the doctor set my arm and wrapped it in a plaster cast, which I had to wear for the next six weeks. First Dad, then me. I guess the Willis boys weren't cut out to be track stars.

When I showed up at school with my arm in a cast, I received a lot of attention and sympathy from the girls. Explaining that I did it while pole vaulting elevated my status among my classmates, and I milked the situation for all it was worth. Sadly, I never again reached that level of coolness during the remainder of my school years.

Dad decided to become a brew master by making and bottling his own beer. He got the recipe from a friend and bought all the necessary equipment and ingredients, including a large glass carboy in which to ferment the beer. When it was ready for bottling, Dad siphoned the amber liquid into glass bottles, capped them, and stored them in a six-foot-tall metal cabinet we kept in our carport. Dad put a lock on the cabinet door and told us not to touch it. He planned on leaving the bottles in there until he was ready to invite his friends over for a beer party.

One afternoon, while Mom was in the kitchen, she heard a loud explosion coming from the carport and peeked out the door. She didn't see anything, so she assumed it was a neighbor's car backfiring. A few minutes later, she heard another explosion and the sound of glass breaking. She peeked out the door again at about the same time that a third explosion shook the cabinet. By this time, she figured out that the beer bottles were exploding.

She called Dad and he rushed home. He must have mistakenly bottled the beer too soon, while it was still fermenting. Dad and I carefully laid the cabinet on its back and gingerly carried it down to the canal. He said he was going to remove the lock and open the door, after which we were going to carefully dump the remaining bottles in the canal. I didn't care too much for that we part, but there wasn't much I could do.

To the uninitiated, it might have looked like some sort of burial at sea ceremony. After we got rid of the bottles (it was dark, so I don't know if they sank or just floated away like a flotilla of torpedoes looking for a target), I was tempted to grab my bugle and play "Taps," but decided against it. The combination of someone playing that piece and lowering into the water a gray, six-foot cabinet that bore a striking resemblance to a coffin immediately after what might be mistaken for gunshots would surely have alerted the local police if not the Federal authorities.

May those sacrificial bottles of home brew rest in pieces. For all I know, the ones that didn't eventually explode could still be bobbing up and down somewhere in the Florida Straits or beyond.

For Christmas, I received the second-best present of my life (golf clubs being the best). I had been pestering my parents to buy me an acoustic guitar ever since my cousin, Rusty, had shown me his the year before. There, under the Christmas tree, was the most beautiful guitar I had ever seen, it's red sunburst finish reflecting the multicolored lights from the tree. Cradling it in my arms, I tuned it and started picking out the notes to The Ventures' "Walk, Don't Run." This guitar was the third big love of my life (after my golf clubs and, of course, Mary).

After Christmas, I ordered several Mel Bay guitar instruction books. I never took formal lessons, but I practiced on that guitar every day until I left home to join the military when I was nineteen. I could tell Mom was relieved that I substituted the melodious guitar for that ear-shattering bugle. I think she threw the bugle away when I wasn't looking.

In December, Dad formally retired as a major from the Air Force. My parents, after considerable thought, decided to settle in Cocoa Beach, a small town up the Atlantic coast near Cape Canaveral. They put down a deposit on a small house close to the beach.

Jan, Buddy, and I were excited and couldn't wait to get there. I was looking forward to seeing rocket launches up close. Then, as so often happened in the Willis household, plans were changed. Dad told me he was having a few beers with Uncle Smoky one night and got to thinking about how he and Mom didn't really know a soul in Florida except for a handful of relatives, while most of his Air Force buddies were retiring in San Antonio.

The next day he got a refund on the house deposit and announced we were heading west to Texas …again. He said Jan and I would have to stay at Grandma's house for a month or two while he, Mom, Becky, Buddy, and John drove to San Antonio. There, he would find a place for us to live.

Before she left, Mom enrolled me in Winter Haven High School. I wasn't too happy knowing I would have to transfer again shortly. The classes and students were different, and I was miserable. A month later, Mom and Dad found a rental house that would be available soon and sent for us. Jan and I said goodbye to a tearful Grandma and flew to San Antonio in February, 1965.

Nine

A Dinner Tale

When Dad was ten years old, he was hanging around the barber shop. Granddad needed to run an errand and asked Dad to watch the shop until he got back; he told him that if a customer came in, ask him to wait until Granddad returned.

A man stumbled through the door, obviously drunk, and demanded a haircut.

"If you'll just have a seat, sir, the Cap'n will be back in a few minutes," Dad said.

"I want a haircut, goddammit," the man replied.

Dad kept insisting that he wait until Granddad returned, but the man would have none of it.

"I don't have time to wait," he said. "I'm sure you can cut my hair as well as your old man can. Now get over here."

Dad was too afraid to argue with the man, so he figured, why not? He had seen Granddad do it a hundred times—how hard could it be?

Dad shook out the bib with a flourish and tied it around the man's neck. He grabbed the clippers and nervously started cutting the man's hair.

After a few minutes, Dad realized it wasn't as easy

as it looked, for the man's head looked as if it had been caught in a fan. With chunks of hair missing, the left side no longer matched the right side. After several attempts to correct his mistakes, he realized he was making things worse.

Finally, the mangy-looking drunk caught a glimpse of himself in the mirror.

Uh, oh, Dad thought to himself. I'm in trouble now.

Instead of getting upset, the man thought the way his hair looked was funny and started laughing. He told Dad he was doing a great job and to keep on cutting. So Dad kept cutting, and the more he cut, the worse it looked, and the worse it looked, the more the man laughed.

After a while, Dad got to laughing. Now both were laughing hysterically, having a grand old time.

Until the door opened and Granddad walked in.

He took one look at his customer and bellowed, "What the hell is going on here?"

The man tried to reassure him that it wasn't Dad's fault, but Granddad hauled off and kicked Dad square in the butt, yelling, "Get your ass home. I'll deal with you later."

After Dad left, Granddad had the job of trying to salvage the man's hair as well as his own reputation.

When Dad picked Jan and me up from the San Antonio airport, I was in a deep funk. As a young boy, constantly being on the move didn't faze me that much, but things were different now. I was a fragile teenager experiencing the physical and emotional extremes of growing up.

Gone were the days when I could move to a new town and fit in with ease and feel a sense of belonging. I first noticed this change when I moved to Winter Haven in January. That was the first time I felt like an outsider. I became a loner—an invisible entity who skirted the social scene like a ghost.

The kids at Winter Haven High School had been very cliquish and seemed to look upon our family with the same suspicion one might harbor toward a band of gypsies who set up camp in their close-knit community. That was when my guitar became my best friend. I had spent most of my evenings doing home-work or holed up in my room pouring my emotional angst into my guitar. I'm sure Grandma must have been a little concerned upon walking in and catching me wiping tears from my eyes as I strummed those melancholy chords.

Grandpa was gone, and with Jan working and Grandma glued to the television, I felt I had no one to talk to or share my innermost feelings. I had been hoping things would change for the better when Jan and I arrived in San Antonio.

This was my fourth move to San Antonio in fifteen years, and I was beginning to feel like a human yoyo. Dad said that as soon as he found a job, he and Mom were going to buy a house. He received a decent pen-sion as a retired major, but with a wife and five kids to feed, it wasn't quite enough to live on.

My parents found a small rental house several blocks from Kelly Air Force Base, near our old friends, the Bordens. Jim Borden retired about the same time as Dad, and his family and ours wasted no time in renewing our old friendship.

Before moving into the rental house, we had to spend a few weeks living in a guest house in Billy Mitchell Village. Since we'd lived there twice before, I had developed quite a sentimental attachment to the old place, despite its rundown appearance.

At the first opportunity, I walked through the neighborhood, trying to locate our two previous apartments. This place was the closest thing to roots I ever had, and I needed that emotional connection like a drunk needed his next drink. I wandered the playground where I got nailed by a swing while stealing my first kiss seven years previously and visited the supermarket parking lot where I had my first brush with fame as a carnival performer (okay, delusions of grandeur might be guiding my hand a little here).

Fond memories came flooding back. I sat on the curb and wondered if I would ever find a real home. Were my parents making empty promises when they said we were finally settling down? San Antonio provided such an important backdrop to my short history that I was desperately hoping this would be my final destination.

At one time, moving was an adventure, but now I needed a lot more than that. I should have talked to Mom and Dad about my confused feelings, but they had problems of their own. For several months, I felt like I was on the verge of an emotional breakdown but was too ashamed to say anything to anyone. Jan might have understood, since we shared many of the same experiences. Mom would have been sympathetic, I'm sure, but Dad would have just told me to be a man and snap out of it.

Enrolling in John F. Kennedy High School didn't do much to ease my anxiety. In addition to being the new kid—again—I experienced something different: culture shock. It didn't take me long to realize I was one of only about ten Anglo kids in a school populated by Mexican-Americans. Most spoke Spanish everywhere, except in the classroom where it was frowned upon by school administrators. When I attended elementary schools in San Antonio, I didn't notice this cultural division. Either the times had changed or maybe little kids don't discriminate.

I have never felt, before or since, prejudice against Mexican-Americans, but it was in my best interest to make friends with the other Anglo kids as quickly as possible. I noticed right away a definite chill toward us. The Mexican-American girls didn't bother me, but several of the boys harassed me constantly, calling me "Guero" and "Johnny Quest" (a popular blond-haired cartoon character). It didn't help that the principal was an Anglo man named Willis who liked to call me "son" in front of the other kids.

Within a month, I got into my first street fight. I was tired of the taunts of one of the Mexican-American boys and confronted him after school one day.

Not a smart move, considering I was outnumbered a hundred-to-one by his buddies in the crowd that had gathered.

No one got hurt, but afterward, I asked Dad if I could transfer to another school, preferably on the north side. He told me to be patient—as soon as he found a house on the north or northwest side of town, we would move and I could change schools.

I needed to earn a little spending money, so I got a job delivering newspapers: the *San Antonio Express* in the morning and the *San Antonio News* in the afternoon. I had to get up at 4:00 a.m. and ride my bike to a retail strip center a mile away, where several other boys and I waited for our delivery of papers from the distributor. We sat cross-legged on the sidewalk and rolled each paper by hand and tied them up with twine. After filling our saddlebags with the papers, we took off into the chill of the pre-dawn darkness.

I usually returned home around 5:30 a.m. and jumped under the covers until 7:00 a.m., when I got up for school. I made up for my lack of sleep by napping through study hall (and when I could get away with it, history class).

After school, I repeated the process with the evening edition. It wasn't an easy job, since I had to memorize two separate routes and deal with irate customers who took exception to my occasionally tossing their paper on the roof (I was a paperboy, not a major league pitcher—plus it was dark). When my bike was stolen one night, my job got even harder.

I had to lug that heavy bag over my shoulder, until Dad felt sorry for me and bought me a new bike.

I got into my second street fight, this time with one of the other paperboys. Two fights within one month didn't make my future in this part of town look too promising. I put pressure on Dad to hurry up and find a house as soon as possible, or he might have one less mouth to feed.

There was a rundown bar in the strip center, and the other boys and I always looked forward to harassing the drunks and hookers who made that area their home at that early hour. It probably wasn't the safest environment for a fifteen-year-old boy, but I was getting quite an education outside of the classroom.

I was probably lucky to get fired after one month. My route manager showed up at my house one day and wanted me to go door-to-door, soliciting new customers. I refused, saying I had all the business I could handle. He told me to either hit the streets or turn in my saddlebags. I told him where he could shove his saddlebags and slammed the door.

In those days, paperboys had to collect subscription fees from their customers in addition to delivering the paper. If a customer refused to pay or managed to never be at home on collection day, the paperboy had to pay the bill out of his own pocket. Today, fees are mailed in, and paperboys drive cars. Things have really changed.

When I was fired, a lot of customers owed me money that I never collected. My net pay for that one month came out to a whopping thirty-five dollars.

That came out to about a dollar an hour. Rockefeller I wasn't, but it was a valuable learning experience.

Dad found a temporary job right away that took him out of the country—again. Even as a civilian, Dad was being taken away from us. He was hired as an aircraft maintenance foreman for a Defense Department contractor—in Okinawa, Japan, of all places. It was only a six-month contract, but the extra income would help him with the down payment on a new house.

We all missed Dad terribly, since we'd thought his globe-trotting days were finally over. I was overjoyed, however, when I came home from school a month after he had left and found him sitting in our living room. I gave Dad a big bear hug and was afraid to let go for fear he would disappear again. I always loved being around Dad, but at this low point in my life, I desperately needed his strong presence more than ever.

Dad explained that everything was going great with his new job until the Japanese government decided to add an additional twenty percent income tax on an already exorbitant tax bill. He gave his notice, as did most of his disgusted fellow workers, and caught the next flight back to the States. That day when I walked in the house and saw Dad sitting on the couch with his arm around Mom was one of the happiest days of my life.

Jan was nineteen and working at Kelly Air Force Base as a secretary. One day she announced she had been accepted for a secretarial position at the Pentagon in Washington, D.C. She was excited and relieved to be finally moving out on her own again. We were a little relieved as well, considering the lack of space in our rental house.

Jan found an apartment in Alexandria, Virginia, near the Pentagon. Several years later, she returned to San Antonio and moved in with us (by this time we had a much larger house). I don't know if she came back because she missed her family, became disillusioned with life in the D.C. area, or had a bad breakup with the Italian guy she had considered marrying.

The only thing she cared to talk about was the time she met President Lyndon B. Johnson. She had been invited to an embassy party, and while standing alone, the President walked up, offered his hand, and asked, "Where's your husband?"

"I don't have one," she stammered, after which the President laughed and walked away.

In September, 1965, Mom and Dad bought their first home at 8022 Latigo Drive on the northwest side of town in the Lackland Terrace subdivision. It was brand new and had four bedrooms and two bathrooms. I thought we were rich. No landlord to appease. No base inspection team looking over our shoulder, ordering us to do a better cleaning job. And enough room for everyone.

I can still smell the fresh paint and concrete dust that permeated the rooms. It was more intoxicating than the scent of any flower or perfume. Mom was flitting from room to room, already mentally organizing and decorating her dream home. Dad was meticulously measuring the walls of the garage for that perfect work bench he had always wanted to build. I was so happy for the both of them. They looked like two kids in a candy store.

I transferred to Oliver Wendell Holmes High School and was relieved to find I wasn't a minority anymore. Since most of our neighbors were retired Air Force families, we fit right in. I made a lot of new friends, including my new best friend, Mike McInnis. He lived several houses down from me and we became inseparable. I was with him the day he met his future wife, Dora, during our senior year.

Mike and Dora were military brats like me. They never talked much about their own vagabond lives, but possibly we sensed in each other that special bond only military kids share. The three of us are still great friends after forty-four years, and we keep in touch on a regular basis. The fact that none of us live more than seven miles from the old neighborhood where we hung out together as kids may be a testament to our desire for permanence and stability.

We had spent fifteen years living in apartments, duplexes, quadplexes, and cracker box houses. I'd figured out by this time I had lived in twenty homes across six states and two countries. Had I finally found my roots? Or was it too late? Kids who get to grow up in the same neighborhood will never understand the uncertainty and frustration of being uprooted every year—the sense of feeling you don't quite fit in, always being targeted as the new kid on the block.

I decided long ago that when I married and had children, I wasn't going to put my family through that ordeal. When Dad later tried to persuade me to pursue a military career, Mom begged me not to do it. She understood the hardships and sacrifices it involved and wanted a better life for me.

Dad once confided to me that his twenty-two years in the military was one long party. It wasn't a party to the Willis kids, and it definitely wasn't a party for Mom. Granted, he was the one risking his life on occasion, but Mom took the brunt of holding a military family together. It was left up to her to provide a stable home life while having to deal with the pressures of packing and unpacking every year and enrolling kids in a seemingly endless succession of schools. I feel every military spouse deserves a special medal and our country's appreciation.

I'm proud of both Mom and Dad for their service to our country. Mom didn't get to wear the same uniform Dad wore. His was the starched and smartly-pressed khakis adorned with the insignia and medals of a decorated officer. Mom's uniform consisted of a worn housedress covered by a flour-stained apron and bobby pins holding her hair in place. Her medals were the clothespins clipped to her apron and the safety pins she clenched between her teeth during her twenty years of changing diapers. They were the crow's feet accenting her eyes that she acquired squinting out the window waiting for the man she loved to return home.

This has been my story. Writing it was one of the hardest things I've ever done. Not so much the mechanics of writing—that was the easier part. Though I have many happy memories from childhood, the hard part was resurrecting some sad and painful times.

My parents weren't perfect, but they did their best with the tools they were given and the unusual circumstances that fate tossed in their path. I loved them immensely and it wasn't until I became an adult and a parent that I understood the overwhelming obstacles they encountered and over which they triumphed.

I did tell them how proud I was of them when they were alive, but I didn't tell them as often as I should have. In retrospect, I realize that, though my parents were persevering and resourceful, they were not unique. Over the years, I have had the privilege of knowing many military families, and I'm sure all of those parents worked just as hard and sacrificed just as much as mine did. I'm also just as sure that they never received a fraction of the recognition they deserved.

Epilogue

As I got older, I discovered a big truth: one's roots are more than a house or a neighborhood or a town. Real roots manifest themselves in the flesh and blood of family and the memories of those who are no longer with us in person but will always be there in spirit.

I failed to realize that my real roots were always with me from the beginning. Disguised in the form of the smile Mom gave me when I came home from school. In the carefree grin Dad flashed when he called me "Tiger." In the unselfish way my grandparents watched me when my parents could not. And the companionship of my brothers and sisters when it seemed the outside world was intent on giving me the cold shoulder.

More importantly, I found that my family consisted of more than just relatives. It consisted of the entire military community. We all watched out for each other and were always there when we were needed.

Despite Mom's resistance, I joined the military in 1969. Dad insisted I apply for appointments to the U.S Military Academy at West Point and the U.S. Coast Guard Academy. I don't know why he was set on my going to one of those two academies. Maybe he figured they were the easiest ones to get into. Dad was very domineering, so I just went along, figuring

I wouldn't hear from either one, and that would be the end of it. Not so. I received an alternate appointment to West Point, but they never called. The Coast Guard Academy did call, however, and offered me an appointment.

I told Dad I didn't want to go (having a girlfriend had a lot to do with it). He told me that if I didn't accept the appointment, I would probably be drafted and sent to Vietnam and he made it clear he wasn't going to send me to college. I chose the Coast Guard Academy, where the biggest risk was getting my butt chewed off by upperclassmen as opposed to going to a jungle halfway around the world and run the risk of getting my butt *shot* off.

After two years, I resigned and returned to San Antonio. Luckily, the Vietnam War was coming to an end. Over the next twenty years, I earned degrees in Business Administration and Electrical Engineering and held a variety of positions in engineering, retail management, and restaurant management. In 1995, I figured I'd had enough of punching a clock for others and decided to become a real estate agent. I enjoy the freedom and will probably do this until I retire.

Along the way, I married a girl named Carrie and started my own family. My two daughters, Katie and Emily, are my proudest accomplishments.

My wife and I bought our first house when Katie was one week old, and lived there for the next seventeen years. I did my best to keep my promise to myself that I would give them the chance to grow up in one neighborhood. Because of a school redistricting problem, we bought another house (when Emily was thirteen) a few miles down the road to ensure both of our daughters went to the same high school. They were still able to keep all their same friends.

Jan married twice before she died of breast cancer in 1987 at the age of forty, leaving behind a husband and five young kids. Buddy, Becky, and John married and started families of their own. Buddy became a carpenter and now owns a successful contracting business. Becky works in the banking industry, at one point holding the position of bank officer. John spent five years in the Navy before returning to college and earning a degree in geology from the University of Texas. He's now a successful geophysicist with an international oil company in Houston.

We all still keep in touch on a regular basis, owing, I'm sure, to the close ties we developed during our frequent moves.

Mom died in 1991 of lung cancer. She was sixty-three. Dad survived heart bypass surgery and lung cancer and lived to the grand old age of eighty-four, dying of natural causes, swinging a golf club right up until the end.

Despite the inconvenience of having to move every year as a kid, I learned—out of necessity—the importance of making friends quickly and adapting to new situations. It also instilled in me a compassion and empathy for others who find themselves in that same social limbo. For that reason, I've always been one of the first to attempt to put a new employee, classmate, or neighbor at ease and do my best to make them feel welcome.

There were some great benefits of growing up on the move, in spite of the rigors. I was fortunate to be able to experience all the great amenities of base life that the government generously provided. I was also privileged to experience a variety of cultures and see parts of the world that most people only read about.

It's not a matter of whether the positives outweigh the negatives. What's important is that what one gets out of an experience is up to the individual. I chose to appreciate the gifts that were given to me rather than dwell on what I might have lost.

The old San Antonio I know is rapidly disappearing. My relatives, who migrated to Houston and Austin years ago, ask me why I stay in San Antonio instead of moving to a town that's more up-to-date and has more to offer. My answer is, they don't know the San Antonio I know. When I drive around San Antonio, I don't see the San Antonio of 2012 with its huge shopping malls, megaplex theatres, golfing resorts, and gated communities. I see the sentimental and historic town of the 1950's and 1960's with its military bases, drive-in theatres, golf courses packed with players lugging their bags slung over their shoulders or using pull carts, mom and pop stores, and kids playing kickball in the streets.

The real estate business has been slow for the past year, so six months ago, I took a part-time job in the lawn and garden department of a Home Depot store. It brings in some extra money and keeps me active.

I'm sixty-two years old now, and one of my last duties at Home Depot on a recent night was pushing a broom across the floor of the outside garden area. It was exactly fifty-two years ago that another sixty-two-year-old man was pushing a similar broom across a Dairy Queen parking lot under the watchful gaze of a ten-year-old boy, grateful for the opportunity to spend time with the man who, while the boy's dad was off "fighting the good fight," filled in as a surrogate father—his beloved Grandpa.

I sometimes feel that my life has come full circle and feel blessed knowing that my kids are proud of me and feel the same love and affection toward me that I felt toward those two men.

Made in the USA
Lexington, KY
27 November 2013